The ✠ guard ✠ The ✠ Seal ✠ of ✠ the ✠ Yeomen ✠ of ✠ the

12   85

The Yeomen of the Guard
1485~1985

The Yeomen of the Guard

FIVE HUNDRED YEARS OF SERVICE 1485~1985

· Julian Paget ·

BLANDFORD PRESS
POOLE · DORSET

First published in the U.K. 1984
by Blandford Press, Link House
West Street, Poole, Dorset, BH15 1LL

Copyright © 1984 Blandford Press Ltd.

British Library Cataloguing in Publication Data

Paget, *Sir* Julian
  The Yeomen of the Guard.
  1. Great Britain. *Army. Yeomen of the Guard*
  —History
  I. Title
  356'11'0941   UA652.Y/

ISBN 0 7137 1157 4

All rights reserved. No part of this
book may be reproduced or transmitted
in any form or by any means, electronic
or mechanical, including photocopying,
recording or any information storage
and retrieval system, without permission
in writing from the Publisher.

Typset by Asco Trade Typesetting Limited, Hong Kong
Printed in Spain by Printer Industria Grafica SA
D.L.B. 26073-1984

Contents

Foreword 6

Preface 7

1 Creation 1485 10

2 'The Nearest Guard' 16

3 The Yeomen Warders 23

4 Protection of the Sovereign 34

5 Yeomen in Battle 44

6 Ceremonial Duties 52

7 Special Body Guard Occasions 67

8 Uniform 84

9 Organisation 92

10 The Standard 101

11 The Yeomen of the Guard Today 105

Appendix A: *The Body Guard in 1485* 116
Appendix B: *Captains of the Guard since 1485* 117
Appendix C: *Chronology of Events 1485 to date* 120
Appendix D: *The Body Guard in 1984* 122
Appendix E: *Body Guard Duties* 125

Acknowledgements 126

Index 127

Foreword

This is the remarkable history of The Queen's Body Guard of the Yeomen of the Guard. It was formed after the Battle of Bosworth in 1485 by King Henry VII as his personal bodyguard and, as he himself stated, it was appointed to uphold the dignity and grandeur of the English Crown and his successors, the Kings and Queens of England, for all time. How splendidly his wishes have been fulfilled!

It is now celebrating 500 years of unbroken service as the personal bodyguard of the Monarch, and is the oldest Royal bodyguard in existence. The duties of the Yeomen in protecting and looking after the personal requirements of the Monarch over the years are very clearly brought out in this admirable narrative—also the fact that they should not be confused with the Yeomen Warders, who are permanently employed as custodians of the Tower of London—a duty they have carried out for many centuries.

The Yeomen of the Guard have always been chosen for their bravery and unswerving loyalty to the Monarch, and since the days of the great Duke of Wellington have been selected from the Armed Forces of the Crown. This history shows how well they have been chosen.

I myself have had the honour of being one of the officers serving with the Yeomen for 18 years, so I have had plenty of personal experience.

I am confident that no finer or more loyal Guard exists in the world today.

Major-General Sir Allan Adair, Bt, GCVO, CB, DSO, MC.
Lieutenant of the Body Guard of the Yeomen
of the Guard 1951–1967

Preface

The Yeomen of the Guard have been the personal bodyguard of the Kings and Queens of England for 500 years, but they are not that well known to the public. Indeed, many people think, wrongly, that they are the same as the Yeomen Warders at the Tower of London.

In fact, the Yeomen of the Guard and the Yeomen Warders are two quite distinct bodies with very different duties, although there are links between them and they do wear almost identical Tudor uniforms. The Yeomen of the Guard are part of the Royal Household and parade as a Royal Body Guard to the Monarch on most State and ceremonial occasions. The Yeomen Warders, on the other hand, have always lived and worked within the Tower, looking after the Royal Fortress itself and guarding whoever or whatever is kept within its walls. They are seen there by some two million tourists each year, and so are inevitably more in the public eye than the Yeomen of the Guard, who appear only on State occasions.

The blame for the confusion must be laid, primarily, at the door of Gilbert and Sullivan, for when they wrote their famous operetta in 1887 about the Yeomen Warders at the Tower, they gave it the misleading title of "The Yeomen of the Guard". Gilbert did think of calling it "The Tower Warders", but then in September 1887 he wrote: 'The more I think of it, the more convinced I am that "The Beefeaters" is the name for the new piece. It is a good, sturdy, solid name...[a] Many years later he explained why, in the end, he changed the title yet again. 'I had christened the piece "The Beefeaters", but Sir Arthur Sullivan considered "The Beefeaters" to be an ugly word; so at his urgent instance the title was altered to "The Yeomen of the Guard".'

The confusion has continued ever since, and there has been no history of the Yeomen of the Guard to put the record straight, except one that was published in 1904 for subscribers only. Theirs is a story that deserves to be told, and it is a great honour and pleasure to me to have been asked to write it.

This book is not intended as the definitive official history recording every detail in chronological order; it is more an account of the people involved, what they have achieved and how they have

carried out their duties during the reigns of no less than 22 Kings and Queens of England.

It is the story of a body of men who have for five centuries been proud to make loyal service to the Monarch and to their country the main purpose of their lives.

Sergeant-Major John Montague, formerly sergeant in the 16th Lancers, from a painting by Sir John Millais, RA. Now in the National Portrait Gallery, London.

Julian Paget

[a] *The First Night Gilbert and Sullivan. Centennial Edition*, edited by Reginald Allen, pp. 307–8

DEDICATED BY GRACIOUS PERMISSION TO
HER MAJESTY THE QUEEN

1

Creation 1485

At dawn on Monday, 22 August 1485, two Kings of England faced each other on a field of battle, just south of the Leicestershire town of Market Bosworth. By sunset the course of English history had been changed dramatically. The Plantagenets had been replaced by the Tudors, and the ruinous Wars of the Roses had ended at last.

On that fateful morning, Richard III, Plantagenet King of England and head of the House of York, commanded an army of 12,000 men, firmly established on the dominating feature of Ambion Hill. He was not an impressive figure, being small and slightly deformed, so that he had acquired the name of 'Crookback'. But he was an experienced and courageous commander, as he had proved at the Battle of Tewkesbury. He was now thirty-three and determined to defend his crown against the hated Lancastrians who challenged him.

About a mile to the west, at Whitemoors on low ground overlooked by the King's army, were the 5,000 men of Henry Tudor, Earl of Richmond, chosen leader of the House of Lancaster. He was only twenty-eight and this was his first real battle, but he was resolute and shrewd, and the throne of England was at stake.

For thirty years now the rival factions of Lancaster and York had divided the country in the bitter struggle for power known as the Wars of the Roses. Thirteen battles had been fought, and over 100,000 lives had been lost. For the last two years Henry Tudor had been in exile in France, but he had never ceased plotting and planning how to overthrow the increasingly unpopular Richard III. He made one abortive attempt at an invasion in October 1483, and it failed. Following that he made several secret visits to Wales to seek the support of those leading families there who were known to favour the Lancastrian cause. On one occasion he was very nearly caught by Richard's troops, and only just escaped from Mostyn Hall, where there is still a secret passage known as 'The King's Hole'.

But by July 1485, all was set for the great gamble, and Henry Tudor assembled his force at Harfleur. It was pathetically small, consisting of only 2,000 or so French mercenaries, with perhaps 500 loyal English supporters, and 'some pieces of artillery' supplied by his ally, the young King Charles VIII of France. He was accompanied as always by the 'private guard of faithful followers' who had remained with him during his exile, and who were soon to become the King's Body Guard of the Yeomen of the Guard.

Henry set sail from Harfleur on 1 August and landed at Milford Haven in his native land of Wales on Sunday, 7 August. His hope was that more supporters would rally to his cause once he had landed, and he was not disappointed.

Once safely ashore, he marched north-eastwards towards Shrewsbury, and was joined at Newtown five days later by the powerful Welsh chieftain Rhys-ap-Thomas, with a welcome 2,000 men.

It was not all so easy however. For example, at Shrewsbury Henry's forces were refused entry into the town by the bailiff, Thomas Milton, who was a staunch Yorkist.

'I have taken an oath,' he declared, 'not to let Henry Tudor enter Shrewsbury except over my body.'

After some parleying, he was eventually won over to Henry's side, but asked, 'How can I go back on my oath?'

'Why, that is easy enough,' he was told. 'Lie down, and the Earl will step over you.'

So it was settled, to the satisfaction of all concerned, and Henry continued his advance, flying his banner bearing the Red Dragon of Cadwallader to show his Welsh descent and to rally his Welsh supporters.

His army had now grown to about 5,000, but one crucial factor remained to be resolved—the attitude of the Stanleys. The two brothers, Lord Thomas Stanley and Sir William Stanley, supported Henry Tudor, but they were not prepared at this stage to commit themselves to fight openly against the King. Apart from anything else, the King held Lord Thomas's son as a hostage and had threatened to kill him if his father proved disloyal. Sir William had already been declared a traitor by the King, and so he was also reluctant to support Henry unless he was fairly sure that the challenger had a good chance of success. That was not yet evident, and so both Stanleys, together with their vital 6,000 men, remained firmly 'on the fence' and kept their options open.

On that morning of the 22nd, the Stanleys could be seen conveniently positioned on the north flank of the battlefield, within sight of both sides and well placed to intervene decisively, if and when it suited them, in support of whichever side they chose.

As dawn broke both armies moved out to their battle positions. Richard III placed his 8,000 bowmen and foot-soldiers on the west slope of Ambion Hill, which he rightly judged to be the likeliest line of advance for Henry; in command he placed John Howard, Duke of Norfolk. Richard himself took command of the cavalry and positioned them on his right flank, nearest the watching Stanleys. The Duke of Northumberland, whose loyalty to Richard was doubtful, was placed in reserve—where in fact he remained and declined to intervene, thus contributing to Richard's defeat.

Henry Tudor assembled his army with the main force in the centre, under the command of John de Vere, Earl of Oxford, an able and experienced soldier. His right wing was guarded by Talbot, and he positioned himself on the very weak left flank. He had expected this to be held by the Stanleys but they had obviously failed him, and without their 6,000 men—including 4,000 horsemen—he was in dire trouble, out-numbered two to one, with virtually no cavalry and in a poor defensive position.

Like many great commanders before and since, he decided that his best form of defence was to attack. But, even as his main body was manoeuvring to move forward up Ambion Hill, Richard III ordered the Duke of Norfolk to attack them while they were still disorganised.

With their far greater numbers and the advantage of charging downhill, the King's men should have swept away the thin lines of Henry's infantry. But the Earl of Oxford calmly ordered his troops to re-group into 'wedges' (not unlike the 'squares' used at Waterloo 330 years later), and they stood firm, the Yorkist cavalry wheeling round them like waves against a breakwater. Fierce hand-to-hand fighting developed, and the Duke of Norfolk was killed. Thwarted and leaderless, the King's men fell back.

For a moment there was a lull in the fighting. But Henry knew he could not win against such overwhelming odds and that his only hope lay in persuading the hesitant Stanleys to intervene on his side before he was worn down by the superior numbers ranged against him. So, in a last desperate bid to win the support of their decisive 4,000 cavalry, Henry Tudor decided he must talk face to face with Lord Thomas. Unfurling his standards and holding them high, so that the Stanleys would recognise him, he set off at a gallop towards them, accompanied only by a small escort of about fifty men.

King Richard from his hilltop could also see the flying standards, and he well realised what was happening.

It was the moment of truth for both of them. Richard had an opportunity to attack and overwhelm Henry and his small party, and at the same time to break through Henry's weak left flank. Such a move would be decisive—provided that the Stanleys did not intervene. If they did, Richard, himself attacked in the flank, would be overwhelmed.

It was a gamble and Richard took it.

Exultantly waving on the 1,000 knights who formed his cavalry, Richard personally led them in a headlong charge down the slope to cut off and destroy Henry's forlorn little party before it could

WARRANT TO THE KEEPER OF THE PRIVY SEAL TO MAKE OUT LETTERS TO THE CHANCELLOR
THAT LETTERS PATENT UNDER THE GREAT SEAL BE ISSUED TO WILLIAM BROWN, YEOMAN OF
THE GUARD TO WHOM THE OFFICE OF BAILIFF OF BRAILES IN WARWICKSHIRE,
HAS BEEN GRANTED. DATED 18 SEPT I HEN. VII.

BY THE KING.

REVEREND FATHER IN GOD. RIGHT TRUSTY AND WELL BELOVED. WE GREET YOU WELL.
AND WHEREAS WE IN CONSIDERATION OF THE GOOD SERVICE THAT OUR HUMBLE AND
FAITHFUL SUBJECT WILLIAM BROWN, YEOMAN OF OUR GUARD, HATH HERETOFORE DONE
UNTO US. AS WELL BEYOND THE SEA AS ON OUR DAY OF VICTORY, AND THAT DURING HIS
LIFE HE INTENDETH TO DO, HAVE GIVEN AND GRANTED UNTO HIM THE OFFICE OF BAILIFF
OF BRAILES IN OUR COUNTY OF WARWICK TO HAVE, OCCUPY AND ENJOY THE SAME OFFICE
UNTO OUR SAID SUBJECT BY HIMSELF OR HIS SUFFICIENT DEPUTY OR DEPUTIES, DURING
OUR PLEASURE. WITH ALL THE WAGES. FEES. COMMODITIES, EMOLUMENTS AND PROFITS TO
THE SAME OFFICE OF OLD TIME DUE AND ACCUSTOMED THEREFORE WE WILL AND CHARGE
YOU THAT UNDER OUR PRIVY SEAL, BEING IN YOUR WARD, YE DO MAKE OUR LETTERS
DIRECTED UNTO OUR CHANCELLOR OF ENGLAND; CHARGING HIM BY THE SAME THAT UNDER
OUR GREAT SEAL, BEING IN HIS WARD, HE DO MAKE OUR LETTERS PATENTS IN DUE AND
SUFFICIENT FORM, ACCORDING TO THE PREMISES AND THESE OUR LETTERS SHALL BE
YOUR SUFFICIENT WARRANT AGAINST US.
GIVEN UNDER OUR SIGNET AT OUR CITY OF LONDON THE XVIII DAY OF SEPTEMBER, THE
FIRST YEAR OF OUR REIGN.

The warrant from Henry VII to his Chancellor requiring letters patent for William Brown, one of the original Yeomen.

reach the ridge where Stanley's men stood watching.

It was a dramatic sight. It was also the crucial moment of the battle. The outcome, so evenly balanced, was to be decided within the next few minutes.

Like a breaking wave, Richard's cavalry struck. The King himself thrust his lance through the body of Sir William Brandon, Henry's standard bearer, and seized the banner. Then, drawing his sword, he joined in the melée of hand-to-hand fighting that must soon, it seemed, bring him victory.

But the moment of truth had also arrived for the Stanleys, and they had now to make their fateful choice between the two sides.

Even so Lord Stanley hesitated, but Sir William, with a shout of '*A Stanley A Stanley*' led his red-coated Cheshire cavalry forward and charged the exposed flank of Richard's force.

The impact was overwhelming, and within seconds the tide of battle had changed.

King Richard was unhorsed by the first onslaught. Another charger was brought and he was urged to escape. But he plunged back into the fray, to be cut down and killed.

It was the end. His army withdrew and fled southwards, pursued by the triumphant Lancastrians. The Wars of the Roses were over.

A weary, but relieved Henry Tudor gathered his forces together and set up his Standard on a small rise to the south, later called Crown Hill. As he thanked and congratulated his companions-in-arms, Sir Reginald Bray appeared, carrying the gold diadem that Richard III had been wearing on top of his helmet, so that he could be easily recognised. It had been found by a soldier in a thorn bush near the spot where Richard fell—the last English King to die in battle.

This famous incident is commemorated in several places by the device of a hawthorn bush with a crown on it. It appears on the Royal coat of arms on the tomb of King Henry VII in Westminster Abbey, and also in the window of his Chapel there, which was completed by his son, Henry VIII. The device also appears on the Standard of the Body Guard.

Crown on the hawthorn bush, c 1509, from the Memorial Chapel at Westminster Abbey.

The crown was handed over to Lord Thomas Stanley, who promptly placed it on Henry Tudor's head, declaring him to be 'Henry VII, King of England'.

Round the King at this moment of triumph were the survivors of that 'private guard of faithful followers' who had endured with him the long years of exile, and who would shortly enjoy the honour of becoming the first permanent Royal Body Guard of England.

The battle over, Henry rested that night near the battlefield and moved on the next day to Leicester. There on 25 August, in the presence of both armies and a gathering of nobles, he was formally proclaimed King of England.

He reached London on 3 September, and promptly attended a Thanksgiving Service in St Paul's Cathedral. On 30 October he was crowned in Westminster Abbey, and was escorted on that great occasion by his Body Guard of the Yeomen of the Guard.

Sadly, there is no documentary evidence as to the exact date on which the Body Guard was officially formed. Indeed, there may never have been any formal document, and their creation may simply have been announced either at the Thanksgiving Service or at the Coronation.

The first written reference to the Guard is in a Royal warrant[1]

[1] There were only five warrants dated earlier than this, one on the 6th, 10th and 15th, and two on the 16th.

dated 16 September 1485, which refers to '... John Frye, one of the Yeomen of the King's Guard...' Another, dated two days later, declares that '... in consideration of the good service that our humble and faithful subject William Brown, yeoman of our guard, hath heretofore done unto us, as well beyond the sea as on our day of victory and that during his life intendeth to do, have given and granted unto him the office of bailiff of Brailes in our county of Warwick...'

It is clear from these warrants that the Body Guard was in existence by 16 September, less than a month after the victory of Bosworth. It seems probable therefore that the King declared actually on the field of battle that his 'private guard of faithful followers' were henceforth to be his Royal Guard, now that he was himself King of England. He is known to have knighted several of his companions in arms on the spot that day, so what more natural than that he should at the same time have made the announcement about his Yeomen, for they were *de facto* his *Royal* Body Guard from that moment.

Whether the precise date be 22 August or some time during the next three weeks, there is no doubt at all that the Yeomen of the Guard date back to 1485, and that they have given unbroken service to the Crown ever since.

The seal of the Body Guard, presented by the Captain, the Earl of Ilchester in 1838 in honour of the Coronation of Queen Victoria.

The King certainly had need of some loyal and reliable personal protection at that moment. There was still considerable turbulence in the country and, as the historian Bacon put it, 'The dissensions of the Yorkists and Lancastrians did ever hang over the Kingdom, ready to break forth into new perturbations and calamities.'

Nevertheless, there was a deep-rooted distrust in the minds of the people of any permanent armed body in the hands of the Crown. King Henry VII was at pains therefore to let it be known that the Yeomen of the Guard were not intended as a threat to anyone, but were, as he memorably described them, 'for the upholding of the dignity and grandeur of the English Crown in perpetuity, his successors, the Kings and Queens of England, for all time.'

They have certainly lived up to that claim made for them five centuries ago.

2

'The Nearest Guard'

On 30 October 1485, Henry VII was formally crowned King of England. This time he received the Crown with all due pomp and ceremony from the Archbishop of Canterbury in Westminster Abbey, instead of amid the chaos and carnage of a battlefield, as at Bosworth.

Standing round him, proudly and protectively on this historic occasion, were his new Guard, making their first public appearance. Fifty of them were there—and we know the names of thirty-eight, which are listed at Appendix A.

At that moment the Yeomen of the Guard held three unique distinctions. First, they were the only Royal bodyguard; second, they were the first *permanent* armed body in the country; third, they occupied the privileged position of being 'the Nearest Guard', that is, those who are entitled to stand nearest to the Sovereign on State occasions.

Previous monarchs had certainly had their personal bodyguards, but these had not been organised on a permanent basis, they had no official title and they usually changed when a new king came to the throne.

The title granted to the Yeomen of the Guard in 1485 was *Valecti Garde (Corporis) Domini Regis*, which is the same title as that used today. Literally translated it means 'Yeomen of the Guard (of the Body) of our Lord the King,' and this is still their full official title.

Through the centuries they have been called 'The King's (or, The Queen's) Body Guard of the Yeomen of the Guard,' the only variation being that during the reign of Queen Victoria the title was changed by her command to 'The Royal Body Guard of the Yeomen of the Guard.' King Edward VII restored the original title as soon as he came to the throne, and so it has remained ever since.

Officers of the Guard

There is little evidence of what officers there were in the Guard in the time of Henry VII. There was certainly a *Captain of the Guard*, and the first one recorded is John de Vere, Earl of Oxford. However, he can have held the post for a few months only, for he was the same year given many other honours, including the

Passing through Admiralty Arch. A detachment of the Body Guard marching in the Coronation procession of King George VI in 1937. The Yeomen have been involved in this impressive ceremony from the Coronation of Henry VII onwards.

appointment of Lord Great Chamberlain. He was at the same time made 'Constable and Keeper of the Lions at the Tower of London,' so he may during his life have commanded both the Yeomen of the Guard and also the Yeomen at the Tower, which is almost certainly a unique distinction.

The Captain in those days had executive command of the Body Guard, and was personally responsible for the safety of the Sovereign at all times, which was a very real task in those troubled days. It was a position of considerable importance and prestige, particularly as at that time, the Captain usually also held the post of Vice Chamberlain. A Royal warrant of 1509, for example, appointed Sir Henry Marney as 'Captain of the Guard and Vice Chamberlain'.

This dual role made sense, because the Vice Chamberlain's duties covered not only security at Court but also the organisation of all ceremonial, as well as the functions now carried out by the

A mounted Yeoman wearing State livery in the time of Queen Elizabeth I. From an engraving by de Bruyn, published in 1575.

Marshal of the Diplomatic Corps. The Captain was often used by the King for particularly delicate diplomatic missions, such as when Sir Charles Somerset (who followed the Earl of Oxford as Captain) was dispatched to Spain in 1505 to negotiate the betrothal of Prince Henry (the future King Henry VIII) to Katherine of Aragon. He seems to have made a success of this particular undertaking, for he was raised to the peerage the following year.

There was almost certainly a *Standard Bearer* in the Guard from the start, although there is no mention of him in the records until 1578, when he appears as receiving a salary of one hundred marks (about £40) a year, which was also what the Captain received.[2]

[2] See the Ordinances and Regulations of the Royal Household under Queen Elizabeth I.

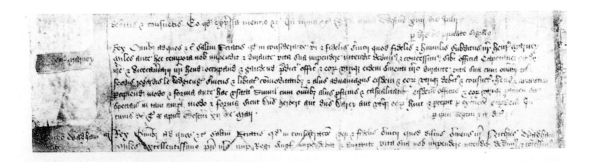

ENROLLMENT OF SIR HENRY MARNEY'S PATENT OF THE OFFICE OF CAPTAIN OF THE GUARD
& VICE-CHAMBERLAIN 12 MAY 1509 [PATENT ROLL I. HEN. VIII. P. II. M. 33]

THE KING TO ALL TO WHOM THESE PRESENTS SHALL COME, GREETING; KNOW YE THAT WE IN CONSIDERATION OF THE TRUE AND FAITHFUL SERVICE WHICH OUR FAITHFUL AND HUMBLE SUBJECT HENRY MARNEY KNIGHT, HAS HERE-TO-FORE RENDERED UNTO US AND DURING HIS LIFE INTENDETH TO RENDER, HAVE GIVEN AND GRANTED TO HIM THE OFFICES OF CAPTAIN OF OUR GUARD AND OUR VICE-CHAMBERLAINSHIP; TO HAVE, OCCUPY AND ENJOY THE AFORESAID OFFICES AND EITHER OF THEM TO OUR SAME SERVANT DURING HIS LIFE WITH ALL SUCH FEES, REWARDS, LODGINGS, SERVICES AND LIBERTIES, COMMODITIES AND OTHER ADVANTAGES DUE AND ACCUSTOMED TO THEM OR EITHER OF THEM; TO HAVE AND TAKE IN MANNER AND FORM HERE-TO-FORE USED, TOGETHER WITH ALL OTHER PROFITS AND CASUALITIES TO THE SAME OFFICES AND EITHER OF THEM PERTAINING OR BELONGING IN AS AMPLE A MANNER AND FORM AS THE LORD HERBERT OR THE LORD D'ARCY OR EITHER OF THEM HAD OR TOOK IN EXERCISE THEREOF. IN WITNESS WHEREOF [WE HAVE CAUSED THESE OUR LETTERS TO BE MADE PATENT] WITNESS THE KING, AT WESTMINSTER, THE 12TH DAY OF MAY.

BY THE KING HIMSELF AND OF THE DATE &c.

Royal warrant of Henry VIII appointing Sir Henry Marney as 'Captain of the Guard and Vice Chamberlain' in 1509.

There are frequent references under the Tudors to the 'standard of the guard', so it seems probable that they had an officer to carry it.

A third officer at this time was the *Clerk of the Cheque*, one of the most ancient appointments at Court, dating back to the fourteenth century. His main duty was to keep a tally of all the staff, his original title being the 'Clerk of the Chequere Rolle'. His duties had little to do with the word 'cheque' in its modern meaning, and he is better described as an Adjutant rather than a Paymaster, though he was at times involved in financial matters.

The first mention of this appointment appears in a Pardon Roll of 1509–1510 where Thomas Broke is shown as 'Clerk of the Check of the Guard' in the King's Household; one, Laurence Eglisfelde was in the same post from 1513, and a certain Bernard Grete held it while the Yeomen were stationed in Tournai from 1513 to 1519. From 1532 onwards we know the names of all those who held this important appointment, and that their salary until 1660 was £20 per annum.

There is no written evidence of there being any other officers in the Body Guard at this time, but an organised body of over 100 men must have had several officers, warrant officers and NCOs, to use modern terms. Any such appointments would have been in the hands of the Captain, which may explain why there is no mention of them in the few State documents covering this period.

There were probably some *Yeomen Ushers* in the Guard, this being a long-established post at Court, equivalent to a warrant officer of today. Indeed, the rank still exists, in that the Guard includes two 'Sergeant-Majors or Yeomen Ushers'.

The bulk of the Guard consisted however of the yeomen, and they deserve detailed mention.

The Yeomen of the Guard

The social structure of England in Tudor times was clearly defined, and the class from which Henry VII formed his Body Guard was described as 'Yeomen or Gentlemen just below the rank of Esquire.' This was an honoured and respected position, linked with the land, but making no pretence to social status on a par with the nobility or the gentry, though many yeomen rose in the world, and became quite wealthy.

A mounted Yeoman of the Guard, leading his horse, c 1625, from an engraving by William van de Passe. 1625.

A good contemporary description of the yeomen comes from the introduction to Hollinshed's *History of Great Britain*:

> *This sort of people have a certaine preheminence and more estimation than labourers and the common sort of artificers (merchants) and those commonlie live wealthilie, keep good houses and travel to great riches... These were they that in times past made all France afraid, and albeit they be not called master, as gentlemen are; or Sir as to Knights appertaineth but onlie 'John and Thomas', etc, yet they have been found to have done verie good worke.'*

The warrant officers and NCOs of the British Army who have comprised the Yeomen of the Guard for the last century and a half are clearly of the same stock.

There were many yeomen at Court in Tudor times, doing a variety of jobs, such as Yeomen of the Kitchen, Yeomen of the Pantry, Larder, Chaundry, the Stables and the Wardrobe; there were Yeomen Tailors and Yeomen Harbingers.

These were probably fairly menial posts, but there were three bodies of yeomen who stood high in the hierarchy and whose appointments were particularly honourable and sought after. They were the Yeomen of the Chamber, the Yeomen of the Crown and the Yeomen of the Guard.

Yeomen of the Chamber had special status because they worked close to the Sovereign, looking after his needs in his private chambers. They were the Royal valets and footmen, and as such they had to be completely trustworthy; their pay was 12*d* a day, like the Yeomen of the Guard, and like them they were in constant attendance at Court.

Yeomen of the Crown in fact pre-date the Yeomen of the Guard, for they can trace their history back to 1419.[3] They were in effect originally a Palace Guard, and King Edward IV (1461–1483) had 24 Yeomen of the Crown in his household. They also looked after Royal prisoners and attended executions, and when King Henry VI was taken prisoner in 1465 he was 'brought through London to the Tower, where he was kept long time by two squires and two yeomen of the crown...'

Another duty for Yeomen of the Crown was to work inside the palaces as guards, and an ordinance of King Henry VII laid down that 'ushers, yeomen of the Crown and yeomen of the Chamber are commanded to set *(sit)* without the chamber door.'

When the Yeomen of the Guard were created, they took over many of these duties, and the importance of the Yeomen of the Crown inevitably declined. The title then tended to be given to any yeomen who were retired or semi-retired from Royal service; they were retained on the Royal payroll and received the standard 'fee of the Crown' which was 6*d* a day and was in effect a form of state pension.

Some were employed on less onerous duties, while others retired completely; they were often allowed to keep their previous accommodation, an early example of 'grace and favour' residences. They wore the distinctive Royal crown on their sleeve and held their title of Yeomen of the Crown for life, in return for which they were liable for recall at any time.

Some Yeomen of the Guard were appointed as Yeomen of the Crown when they retired and they then became known as 'Yeomen of the Guard and of the Crown'. Certainly when King Henry VIII had to economise and reduced the strength of the Guard from 600 to 200, he arranged that most of those declared redundant became Yeomen of the Crown.[4]

Dress. The Yeomen of the Guard did not look as impressive in the time of King Henry VII as they do today. Their everyday wear was an outfit of 'russet cloth', which was a practical order of dress for their role of fighting men engaged in the full-time protection of the Sovereign. Their jackets bore a Tudor rose on the front and back, and their headdress was a black, beret-style cap. In battle they

---

[4] It is possible that the establishment for Yeomen of the Crown was only 24, and that there were others who had the title but no pay. The appointment seems to have died out sometime after.

probably wore light armour on their shoulders, and perhaps a helmet.

About half the Body Guard were mounted in Tudor times, and these men provided an escort for the Monarch either on his travels or in battle. They wore the same uniform as the Yeomen on foot, though their weapons were different.

The Yeomen did have a ceremonial livery for use at Court. This was white and green (which were the Tudor colours, although the Royal colour was always scarlet). The Wardrobe Accounts of 1497 contain an entry for the Guard of '24 jackets of white and green, with guards white and green'.

A State version of this uniform was worn at the marriage of Prince Arthur and Princess Katherine on 14 November 1501, and was described as being 'of damask white and green, goodly embroidered both on their breasts before and also on their backs behind, with round garlands of vine branches, beset before richly with spangles of silver and gilt, and in the middle a red rose, beaten with goldsmith's work...'

They carried swords and also bows and arrows, for they were primarily archers. In addition they were equipped with the standard weapon of a foot soldier of that time, which was a pike. For ceremonial duties, however, they carried a *partisan*, a tapered spear, some 7ft long, with wings at the base of the blade and decorated with a tassel in Tudor green and white. The same weapon is still carried today by the Yeomen, though the tassel is now red and gold.

The partisan is easily confused with the *halberd*, which was another weapon of the sixteenth century, but with an axe-head so that it could be used for cutting and slashing as well as stabbing. Halberds may have been issued to the Yeomen at some stage, but their main weapon was the partisan.

The Yeomen lived at Court, with their food, lodging and clothing all provided, so by the standards of the day they were well looked after. Their basic pay was 12*d* a day when in attendance on the Monarch, with a reduction to 8*d* at other times, as for example when certain Yeomen received this for 'attending on the Queen'. They also received a pension of 4*d* to 6*d* when they retired.

During the reign of their founder, Henry VII, the Yeomen were the only Royal bodyguard, and enjoyed the honour and privilege due to them for their loyalty to him during his exile and on his return to England. There were to be several changes—for better and worse—when his son, Henry VIII, came to the throne.

3

The Yeomen Warders

On the morning of 11 July 1939, King George VI inspected His Body Guard of the Yeomen of the Guard in the grounds of Buckingham Palace. That same evening, at the Sadler's Wells Theatre in London, there was a performance of Gilbert and Sullivan's popular operetta *The Yeomen of the Guard*, which is set at the Tower of London. But this was not about the same people.

The *Times* devoted its leading article the next day to the anomaly, and summed up the popular confusion neatly (if not entirely accurately):

'... *when Gilbert posted his Yeomen of the Guard in the Tower of London it is as likely as not that he knew he was wrong. The Corps of Tower Warders are not, strictly speaking, Yeomen of the Guard. They wear almost exactly the same uniform and they are an offshoot of the main body, but they are "Extraordinary of the Guard" ... they have their special duties and they take no part in the ceremonial functions of the Guard proper. The corps dates only from 1509–10, when King Henry VIII gave up the Tower as a residence, but, in order to maintain it as a royal fortress, left there a separate corps of twelve men detached from the Body Guard formed by his father, King Henry VII, in 1485. That would make a nice little trap in a general knowledge paper ...*'

One of the main causes of the widespread confusion is that the two bodies do wear 'almost exactly the same uniform'. But there is one vital difference; the Yeomen of the Guard wear a gold embroidered cross-belt over their left shoulder, and the Yeomen Warders do not. This belt was originally used in the sixteenth century to carry the arquebus or musket which was at that time the main weapon of the Body Guard in battle. The Yeomen of the Guard were fighting men, protecting the Sovereign, whereas the duties of the Yeomen Warders kept them virtually confined to the Tower of London, looking after the Royal palace and fortress, and its contents.

There have been warders of some sort at the Tower since William the Conqueror started to build it in 1078, and their duty was to guard the State prisoners who were confined there, particularly in Tudor and Stuart times. Their first recorded captive, Bishop Flambard of Durham, in fact escaped by sliding down a rope that

was smuggled in to him in a cask of wine. But thereafter there were few escapes, and the successful ones were notably ingenious.

The warders were also responsible for locking the main gate of the Tower every night, a routine that is still carried on today in the traditional Ceremony of the Keys. This task was in the hands of the Yeoman Porter, and it is recorded that in 1360 King Edward III made a 'Grant for life to the king's armourer John de London of the keeping of the gate of the Tower of London, he taking in the keeping 4*d* a day and the fees pertaining thereto, and 2*d* a day for himself and another 2*d* a day for the wages of a yeoman for the time wherein he and the yeoman be occupied about the mak-

An early photograph of Yeomen Warders at the Tower of London. There have almost certainly been Yeomen Warders on duty at the Tower of London for some 900 years.

ing of the king's harness and armour there and not otherwise occupied...'

The custody of the gate—there was then only one land entrance—was thus not to be in the charge of one of the soldiers of the Tower garrison, but was entrusted to a selected Royal employee who held the post for life and had a yeoman to help him. It may be fairly said therefore that John de London is the direct ancestor of the Chief Yeoman Warder of today, while his assistant is the equivalent of the Yeoman Warder acting as Watchman at night. The Byward Tower, which he and others before him have used since 1280, is still the Watchman's base today.

There seem to have been throughout the history of the Tower two distinct bodies responsible for its security; a permanent staff of Yeomen Warders for the gates and the custody of prisoners, and a garrison of soldiers changing over at intervals. In 1460, for example, a nominal roll shows a garrison of 21 men at arms, 36 archers and 8 crossbowmen. Today their place is taken by the men of the Tower Guard, usually provided by the Foot Guards.

Until the sixteenth century the Tower was the Sovereign's State residence in the capital, and whenever Henry VII stayed there some of the Yeomen would have been with him for his personal protection. He would, of course, have had other staff there as well to look after him, and we know, for example, from an entry dated 31 October 1505 in the King's Book of Payments, that he paid £29.18s.0d in 1505 for 'xiii yomen of the Chambre attending at the tower of London for their quarter wages ended at michell last ...'

The Royal accounts for 1508 show that 'watching clothing' was issued for twelve 'Yeomen of our crowne and chambre giving their attendance by our commandment within our Tower of London.' The names include two individuals, John Williams and William Madock (or Maddockes), who can both be identified as former Yeomen of the Guard, who had by then perhaps retired and become Yeomen of the Crown.[5]

This is largely conjecture, but it is known that when Henry VIII came to the throne in 1509 he stationed twelve Yeomen of the Guard permanently at the Tower; they were known as 'Yeomen of the Tower', and presumably carried out the duties of Yeomen Warders, as opposed to those of the Body Guard. They were paid 6d a day, and apparently took their orders from the Captain of the Guard as well as from the Lieutenant of the Tower. (One of their number was apparently made senior to the others, for there are several references in Henry VII's reign to 'Olyver Turnour and xi of his fellows …')

Thus the link between the Yeomen of the Guard and the Yeomen Warders can be traced back to 1509 though the Yeomen Warders evidently did not wear the Royal livery at this time.

A key date in the history of the Yeomen Warders is 1549, for on 6 October in that year, Edward Seymour, Duke of Somerset and Lord Protector of the Realm during the minority of his nephew, King Edward VI, was arrested on the orders of the King for treason and sent to the Tower. He was apparently well looked after by the Yeomen Warders, with far-reaching results, as described in the Tower Records:

'He noticing the daily and diligent attention of the Warders of the Tower, did out of an honourable mind to encourage them, promise them that when it please God and the King to deliver him out of prison, he would procure that favour from the King, that they should wear his crown as the Yeomen of the Guard did. The Duke not long after being set at liberty, performed his promise and caused the Warders of the Tower to be sworn 'Extraordinary of the Guards' to wear the same livery as they do, which had this beginning in this manner, and has ever since been continued.'

So, in 1550, when the Duke was released, 15 Yeomen of the Tower were duly sworn in as 'Extraordinary Yeomen of the Guard'. They were also given the same uniform as the Body Guard, *except* for the cross-belt, which was clearly not needed on practical grounds, as they would never be equipped with the ar-

[5] John Williams is mentioned in 1503 and William Madock was one of the original Yeomen in 1485.

26

The Chief Yeoman Warder closes the gate to the Tower of London as part of the ancient Ceremony of the Keys in 1898.

quebus. So it is that the two bodies wear 'almost exactly the same uniform'.

Queen Elizabeth did not use the Tower as a Royal residence, though she followed the custom of staying there before her Coronation. So the palace buildings there fell into decay, and for the next two hundred years the Tower became primarily a prison – the garrison of professional soldiers had left – with the Yeomen Warders looking after its security and that of its inmates, and the Yeomen Porter closing the gate each night.

Then, in 1580, a report was prepared to see whether any economies in manpower could be achieved at the Tower (times do not change!). The report pointed out that '... a number of tall Yeomen of the Chamber and the Guard live on her Majesty's wages, hanging daily on the Court, where they may be spared ... and that the great part of the Yeomen of the Tower, now being, are, for age and sickness, feeble, old and not qualified to serve there.'

It then goes on (in tones that might be heard at a Trade Union conference of today) '... specially considering this hard world, in which a Yeoman cannot sufficiently live under 8d ... for they be near hard-pinned and have not clothes to their back.'

The recommendation finally made in the report was that some of the fit, under-employed Yeomen of the Guard should be drafted to the Tower to reinforce the hard-pressed Yeomen Warders; it would then be possible to dispense with some of the soldiers still there and so achieve an overall economy. This seems to have been done, and a number of Yeomen of the Guard were sent to the Tower 'to watch and ward' until about 1601. This practice supports the theory that the formalising of the Yeomen Warders arose in the first place from the early Tudor drafts of older Yeomen of the Guard being transferred to the Tower as Yeomen Warders.

Yeomen of the Guard were naturally appointed in the first place by the Captain of the Guard, and he seems originally to have nominated the Yeomen Warders too. Then in 1624 the Lieutenant of the Tower, Sir Allan Apsley, tried to appoint some Tower Warders himself while the Captain of the Guard was abroad. He used as his pretext the 'danger of admitting those chosen by another'. But when the Captain heard of this on his return, he promptly appealed to the King, declaring that, 'Having command of the King's person, I may be trusted with that of his prisoners.' He won his point, and his right to appoint Yeomen Warders was confirmed. The Constable of the Tower was later given the power to choose his own Warders, possibly by Charles II when he reorganised the Royal Household in the 1660s.

In 1683, following a complaint by the Yeomen Warders about overdue backpay, the Master General of His Majesty's Ordnance, Lord Dartmouth, was ordered to prepare a report about the organisation at the Tower. He found that since 1672 there had been on the establishment '40 Yeomen of the Guards Warders of the Tower, whose pay came to £851.13s.4d per annum.'[6] He also described several malpractices that had developed over the years. For a start, the officers and Yeomen were both making an income by selling their appointments and, in addition, they were letting their quarters in the Tower to civilians while they themselves lived elsewhere. Finally, they were taking up other jobs, indulging in other words in some 'moonlighting'.

Lord Dartmouth recommended among other things that the number of Yeomen Warders should be reduced 'as they die off' to a maximum of 24, as this was the number of quarters available in the Tower. The King approved the report and carried out the recommendations mentioned, except that he did not solve the problem of the purchase of appointments.

This was quite a profitable trade, for if a Yeomen Warder retired he could expect to get some 250 guineas for his post. But if he died while still a Warder, this purchase money was taken by the Constable of the Tower. Hence the traditional toast, which is still drunk today when a new Warder is installed, 'Yeoman Warder, may you never die a Yeoman Warder!' This is known as the Cere-

---

[6] There were 40 in 1667, later reduced to 20, but raised to 40 again in 1672.

mony of the Punch Bowl, the punch being ladled from a pewter bowl of 1724, bearing the Royal arms.

The practice of purchase continued until the nineteenth century when the Duke of Wellington, who was Constable of the Tower from 1826 to 1852, made two major changes. He abolished the sale and purchase of Yeomen Warder vacancies, and in 1827 he also decreed that all the Yeomen Warders should no longer be civilians, but should, like the Yeomen of the Guard, be recruited from deserving ex-soldiers who had held the rank of sergeant or above. This has since been modified to include members of the Royal Marines and the RAF, provided they (like those from the Army) hold the Long Service and Good Conduct Medal; all are now former warrant officers or colour sergeants.

The Yeomen Warders Today

Today the Yeomen Warders are one of the best-known sights in Britain, as they show up to 15,000 visitors a day round the Tower of London. There are between 35 and 40 of them, headed by the *Chief Yeoman Warder*, who inherits the ancient and honourable post of Porter of the Tower and carries as a symbol of his office a ceremonial mace, topped by a silver model of the White Tower.

At some stage the post of Yeoman Porter was upgraded to the dignity of Gentleman Porter, and a petition dated 22 September 1524, describes Robert Leighton as 'gentleman porter Tower of London and Yeoman of the Crown', while in 1582 the post was held by 'one Sir William Gorges (a decayed and poor knight)'. In 1714 a Yeoman Porter was appointed as well, and by 1853 the post of Gentlemen Porter had become a sinecure.

The next senior in the Body of Yeomen Warders is the *Yeoman Gaoler*, who has always had the responsibility of supervising the prisoners and also their guards. He carries a ceremonial (not an executioner's) axe which was traditionally held in front of prisoners when they were escorted from the Tower to Westminster and back for their trials. On the way there, the blade was held pointed away from the accused, but if he or she was found guilty, it was turned round to face them on the return journey—a simple way of announcing the verdict to the public. There have been Gentlemen Gaolers too and the last one died in 1861.

The *Yeomen Clerk* has been added more recently to the senior ranks, and runs the extremely busy office in Queen's House. Only these three carry the keys.

The 'Yeomen Waiters or Warders of the Tower',[7] to give them their full title, have at various times been responsible for the cus-

---

[7] The duty roster is still called *The Wait*.

Inspection of the Yeomen Warders in 1898. The Chief Yeoman Warder, first left, is carrying the ceremonial mace which is topped by a model of the White Tower.

tody of many things besides prisoners, for the Tower has housed not only kings and queens and the Crown Jewels, but also astronomers, arms and armour, coinage of the realm, State records, and animals and birds. For nearly 500 years (1344–1811) the Royal Mint was established there, and the Royal Observatory was there too; stocks of ammunition and explosives have been stored within its walls, and as recently as 1835 it even contained a Royal menagerie. Then one of the lions bit a sentry, whereupon the animals were hurriedly transferred to Regents Park, where they joined the Zoo that had been set up there some nine years before.

One of the Yeomen Warders, the *Yeoman Raven Master*, looks after the famous Tower ravens. Their presence dates back to the time of Charles II, when the Astronomer Royal complained to the King that the wild ravens were interfering with his work. The King agreed to their destruction, but was then told of the belief that if the ravens left the Tower of London, the White Tower would fall and so would the Kingdom; he therefore decided to leave a limited number, just to be sure, and the tradition has continued. In fact for a short while in 1946, there were no ravens at the Tower, but both it and the Kingdom survived; though it could be said that 1946 marked the beginning of the end of the British Empire! In any case, there are now six ravens officially 'on the establishment', with two in reserve, and they are fed at a cost of £1.00 per week by the Yeoman Raven Master.

Until 1967 the Yeomen Warders were also responsible for the Crown Jewels, but then a new Jewel House was completed and a separate body of curators and wardens was set up to take over this duty.

The post of Yeoman Warder used to be for life, but Warders now retire at the age of 65. They are selected by the Constable of the Tower, on the advice of the Resident Governor, and the latter swears them in as Yeomen Warders. They are also sworn in as special constables and carry out the duties of the police within the Tower, since the Metropolitan Police do not enter the Tower on duty except with the permission of the Governor. Finally, they are sworn in for a third time, on this occasion as 'Yeomen Extraordinary to the Guard', thus maintaining the precedent that was established in 1550.

Unlike the Yeomen of the Guard, the Yeomen Warders are employed and paid full time, and they live at their place of work. In 1952 they were made civil servants and as a result they now belong to a trade union and have on occasion been called out on strike, much to the delight of the cartoonists: they have, however, always steadfastly carried out their main security duties, even when officially on strike.

The Beefeaters

The Yeomen Warders are widely known as *The Beefeaters*, though this ancient nickname is not popular either with them or with the Yeomen of the Guard to whom it is also applied.

There is some uncertainty as to the origins of the term, and one theory is that it is derived from the French word *buffetiers*, i.e. those who served at the Royal buffet, but this is an unlikely answer. Much more probable is that the Yeomen have always been hearty eaters of beef. In 1669, for example, Count Cosmo d'Medici, son and heir of the Grand Duke of Tuscany, paid a state visit to England and wrote an account of his travels.[8] He saw the Yeomen of the Guard and said of them, 'They are called "Beefeaters", that is, eaters of beef, of which a considerable portion is allowed daily by the Court.' This was certainly true, and even as late as 1813 the ration for the 30 Yeomen on duty at St James's Palace was 24 lb of beef a day! In comparison the other meat supplied was a mere 18 lb of mutton and 16 lb of veal.

The Yeomen of the Guard were undoubtedly good trenchermen, for in addition to their substantial meat ration they had a daily allowance of 37 gallons of beer for 30 men. On the special occasions such as Royal birthdays when the entire Guard, 81

---

[8] *Travels of Cosmo the 3rd through England*, 1669.

strong, were on duty together, the issue was an impressive 216 lb of meat, 144 loaves, 104 gallons of beer and 240 quarts of wine. They also had Royal venison twice a year, five geese at Michaelmas and three plum puddings every Sunday. So they did feed right well at Court, and must have been sorry when this privilege ceased in 1813 and they were given an allowance of 3s 9d per day in lieu.

An improbable but entertaining tale as to how the Yeomen came to be known as 'beefeaters' relates to King Henry VIII, who liked to disguise himself as an ordinary citizen and then move incognito among his subjects. Once, while on a hunting expedition near Reading Abbey, he dressed up as a Yeoman and paid a visit to the Abbot about dinner-time. He was invited in to the meal, which featured a large joint of beef, and the King, being 'hungry as a hunter' ate heartily of it.

The Abbot watched enviously and then raised a glass to his unknown guest. 'Fare well thy heart,' he declared. 'And here in a cup of sack I remember the health of His Grace, your master. I would an hundred pounds if I could eat as heartily of beef as you. Alas! My weak and squeamish stomach will hardly digest a piece of a small rabbit or a chicken.'

A few weeks later the Abbot was suddenly seized, without knowing why, and thrown into the Tower. For weeks he lived on the usual prison diet of bread and water, until one day, to his surprise and delight, a joint of beef was put in front of him. He attacked it with gusto, and while in the middle of it, the door opened and in came the King, demanding his hundred pounds for having restored to the Abbot his lost appetite for roast beef!

The Abbot paid up gladly and was promptly released. Ever thereafter, whenever he saw a Yeoman of the Guard, he recalled the incident, and told the tale so many times that it finally became accepted that all Yeomen were Beefeaters.

There are in fact many references in literature from the seventeenth century onwards to the Yeomen as great 'eaters of beef', and there seems little doubt that this is the origin of the nickname of Beefeaters, which has remained with them ever since.

The Yeoman Gaoler with his ceremonial axe.

Ceremonial Duties

The Yeomen Warders do not today take part in any State ceremonial occasions except for coronations, when they have the privilege of forming a Guard of Honour inside the Annexe of Westminster Abbey. This is the only time they are on parade at the same time as the Yeomen of the Guard, except when the latter are inspected every fourth year by the Monarch, and eight Yeomen Warders then 'keep the base' for the parade.

The Yeomen Warders were, however, called upon quite fre-

1 The Queen and Prince Philip, with members of the Royal Family, pass through a guard of Yeomen, at the State Opening of Parliament, 1970.

2 Field of the Cloth of Gold, thought to be by Holbein. King Henry VIII, guarded by his Yeomen, prepares to enter the castle at Guines. In the background to the right of the picture the Yeomen can be seen carrying dishes into the Royal tent. The Yeomen with the King are marching in threes, each armed with a sword and partisan.

3 Embarkation from Margate in 1613 of Princess Elizabeth, daughter of James I, and her husband the Elector Palatine. In the foreground are Yeomen trumpeters, two in black hose and one in white. From a painting by Adam Willaerts, 1623.

4 In the past the Yeoman Gaoler had the task of supervising the Tower's prisoners and their guards. He carries a ceremonial – not an executioner's – axe as his symbol of office.

5 The Yeoman Raven Master of the Yeomen Warders of the Tower of London. There are currently six ravens 'on the establishment' with two in reserve. Their presence dates back to the time of Charles II.

6 *Opposite:* The Chief Yeoman Warder is the Porter of the Tower of London and carries his fine ceremonial mace as the symbol of his office. The mace is topped with a model, in silver, of the White Tower.

7 Two Messenger Sergeant-Majors. The Senior Messenger Sergeant-Major *left* lives at
St James's Palace and is responsible for the administration of the Guard, the correspondence
and the keeping of all rosters and records. He also acts as Wardrobe Keeper.

quently in the seventeenth and eighteenth centuries to help out the Yeomen of the Guard in their ceremonial duties. A notable instance was the trial of Lord Ferrers in 1760, when the Captain of the Guard, Lord Falmouth, wrote to the Constable of the Tower, the Earl Cornwallis, requesting that '... 12 Yeomen Warders of the Tower of London in Ordinary, being Yeomen of the said Guard Extraordinary, attend at the Court of Requests in Westminster Hall on 16th April next.'

The Constable declined the invitation on the grounds that all his Yeomen Warders were already involved in guarding and escorting[9] the accused. Lord Falmouth replied confirming his right to the services of the Yeomen Extraordinary when he considered it necessary for extraordinary occasions, but he agreed to excuse them the duty this time. He later demanded 30 Yeomen Warders for the funeral of King George II, and they were provided without demur.

The Yeomen Warders do not wear their State dress outside the Tower except for a coronation or for the Inspection of the Body Guard. Within the Tower it is worn on the three traditional feast days of Easter, Whitsun and Christmas, and also on special occasions such as when a Royal salute is fired there, at the installation of the Constable of the Tower, and for the ancient ceremony of Beating the Bounds. They are also allowed to wear it if a child of a Yeoman Warder is married in the Chapel Royal of St Peter ad Vincula, which is within the Tower walls.

Everyday wear is a blue undress uniform introduced in 1858, and at night those on duty still wear scarlet 'watch coats', similar to those issued by King Henry VII.

There have almost certainly been Porters and Yeomen Warders on duty at the Tower of London for some 900 years, and the Yeomen Warders' Hall in the South Byward Tower has been in continuous use by them for the last 700 years.

The Body of Yeomen Warders can thus claim to be one of the oldest corps in the world still carrying out their original duties. In their capacity as special constables they are still charged with the security and control of access to the Tower, as well as looking after its two million visitors a year. Long may the Yeomen Body continue to guard this ancient Royal Palace and Fortress.

[9]The Constable later submitted a bill for the work involved, which read:

	£	s	d
To safe keeping Lawrence, Earl Ferrers, 11 week and 3 days	26	6	7½
April 16th—to carrying said Lawrence, Earl Ferrers to Westminster Hall	2	0	0
April 17th—to ditto	2	0	0
April 18th—to ditto	2	0	0
April 18th—to carrying said Lord F ... to Tower Hill	2	0	0
	8	0	0

4

Protection of the Sovereign

From the start, the primary role of the Body Guard was the protection of the Sovereign. This was a formidable task, for they were responsible for security 24 hours a day, inside and outside the Royal palaces, at home and abroad, in war and in peace. The threat to the Monarch was very real in those days, for the Sovereign faced not only foreign enemies and agents, but also rivals, pretenders and ambitious nobles at home.

Responsibility for this protection rested with the Captain of the Guard, who was therefore chosen with some care, particularly as far as his loyalty and discretion were concerned. It could be a delicate tight-rope to walk. In 1553, for example, the Captain, Sir John Gates, marched against Mary Tudor on the orders of Lady Jane Grey, who was then Sovereign. Two weeks later, he was escorted to the Tower by his own Yeomen and executed—by order of the new Queen, Mary! In 1549, Sir Anthony Wingfield had to arrest the Lord Protector of the Realm, the Duke of Somerset, and escort him to the Tower, while Sir Walter Raleigh twice found himself being escorted by his own Yeomen to captivity in the Tower.

The Captain had to provide protection not only for the Sovereign but also for the Royal Family and, in 1492, for example, a detachment was detailed by Henry VII to attend on the Queen Consort. She seems to have appreciated their care, for when one of them, Yeoman Griffiths, died, she arranged for him to be buried at St Margaret's Westminster, and paid for his funeral expenses which amounted to 27 pence.

This demanding duty, of protecting the Sovereign every hour of the day, was gradually reduced over the years. King Henry VIII created another Royal bodyguard in 1509, whom he called the 'Gentlemen Spears', and they shared in the responsibility. The Yeomen did not give up any of their existing duties, but were reinforced by the Gentlemen Spears who, because they were all mounted, were particularly useful as a mounted escort in battle and on Royal progresses round the country.

In 1539, the Gentlemen Spears were given the new title of Gentlemen Pensioners, probably copying the French royal guard who were called *Pensionnaires*, that is, those who ate at the King's table or *pension*. An example of how they shared the duty of protecting the Sovereign with the Yeomen comes from an Order in Council in

Primitive woodcut print from a seventeenth-century chapbook, illustrating the tale of the King and the cobbler. King Henry VIII, who loved to disguise himself, visited a cobbler dressed as a Yeoman of the Guard. The cobbler later returned the call, and found to his horror that his new friend was the Monarch.

the time of Charles I which declared that 'as often as His Majesty did ride abroad the Captain of the Yeomen of the Guard and Lieutenant of his Pensioners should ride continually near His Majesty's person and suffer none of mean condition, or unknown to them, to come near.'

In 1661, when Charles II created his standing army, it included three troops of Royal Guards (later to be called The Life Guards), who became the first Household Cavalry; from then on they provided nearly all the Royal mounted escorts, thus relieving both the Royal bodyguards of this responsibility.

The Life Guards also provided officers who had the duty of 'attendance on the King's person on foot, wheresoever he walk, from his rising to his going to bed ...' This did not, however, cover the time he was *in* bed, and here the Yeomen of the Guard took over and carried out the ritual called 'The Service of All Night'.

A detailed account of this elaborate ceremony was written by one of the Esquires of the Body of King Charles II called Ferdinand Marsham, and it is worth quoting:

'The Gentlemen Usher Daily Waiter having the charge of constant attendance upon his Majesty until nine o'clock at night,

Left: Yeomen of the Guard as they appeared during the reception of Marie de Medici in 1639.

A Yeoman from the time of King George II.

called to the Yeomen Ushers [from the Body Guard] attending at the Guard Chamber Door for the Yeoman to attend him for 'All Night' for the King. The Gentleman Usher went bare-headed, and the Yeoman, to the pantry for bread, to the buttery for two flagons of beer, to the spicery for sugar, nutmeg, etc, to the wine-cellar for two great flagons of wine, and drank the King's health in both cellars, causing all to be uncovered, going back, and having a Groom of the Chamber carrying a lighted torch before the Gentleman Usher until he returned into the Presence Chamber, and lay all the services upon the cupboard there, and so deliver all to the Esquire of the Body and took his leave. The Esquire then took the inner keys and charge of 'All Night', called to the Yeoman Usher or Clerk of the Cheque for the Roll of the Watch, and the Page of the Presence with a silver basin with a wax mortar [a night lamp] and sizes attended the Esquire into the Privy Gallery. Then he took the basin, etc, and carried it to the King's bedchamber and stayed until his Majesty went to bed, and then went himself to bed under the state in the Presence Chamber in a pallet-bed sent up from the wardrobe.'

The *Exon in Waiting* who was in command of the detachment of the Yeomen of the Guard on duty used to sleep on a pallet-bed outside the door of the King's bed-chamber, so positioned that no-one could enter without moving the bed and so waking him up.

The task of protecting the Monarch remained a very real responsibility for the Body Guard, and there were several attempts on the life of the Sovereign that were dealt with by the Yeomen. Three plots were hatched to assassinate King William III, but all were thwarted because he was always so closely escorted by Yeomen of the Guard. A fourth attempt, planned for 15 February 1696, might well have been successful had it not been discovered in time. The plan on this occasion was to attack him while he crossed the Thames at Queen's Ferry after a hunting trip in Richmond, and he would then have been unprotected, as the Yeomen had to be left on the bank while the King crossed.

Three attempts were also made on the life of King George III, and in each case the Yeomen helped to protect him. On 2 August 1786 a cryptic entry appears in the Body Guard records, 'Attempt to stab the King by Margaret Nicholson, Insane Woman. Saved by Yeoman of the Guard Francis Kerridge.'

Then, on 15 May 1800, the King was attacked while attending a Review in Hyde Park. He went nevertheless to Drury Lane Theatre that same evening, only to have a pistol fired at him by a man in the audience. The bullet missed, passing between the two Yeomen on duty, who promptly seized the offender. It is largely as a result of this that the Body Guard still escort the Sovereign at Royal Gala performances at the Royal Opera House, Covent Garden in London.

A major change in the arrangements for the protection of the Monarch came in 1813 when the Yeomen ceased to live at Court, and so were no longer all constantly on duty, but had one Division only in attendance at a time. Then, in 1834, Sir Robert Peel formed the Metropolitan Police who took over responsibility for most of the security of the Royal Family.

But this was not quite the end of the matter, for when the Chartist Riots broke out in London in 1848 the Body Guard were summoned to protect the Royal palaces from the mob. The Yeomen were issued with 'Percussion Musquets and Rammers and Bayonets' and were drilled as a company every day except Sunday. On 10 April and again on 12 June they were placed under arms, ready for any emergency; but in the end they were not called on, and were, somewhat reluctantly, dismissed.

Even in this century a member of the Body Guard has helped to protect the Sovereign as part of his duty. On 29 January 1908, as King Edward VII was returning from the State Opening of Parliament, a suffragette ran towards his carriage, shouting 'Petition ... Petition.' According to reports, 'She would have reached the coach, had not Yeoman Allan Wood, who was marching alongside the near front wheel, seized and held her until the police came up and removed her.'

The protection of the Sovereign has involved a remarkably wide range of duties, some of which still survive today, five centuries later.

Lining the Approaches

The Body Guard have always guarded the doors to the Royal ante-chambers and also lined the approaches to the audience chambers, and they still do so today on State occasions. Charles I laid down in his Household Book:

> 'Above stairs the Yeomen of Our Guard are to attend in Our Great Chamber as hath been accustomed. And because their service importeth not only the safety of Our person, but the honor of Our Court, we ordain that none hereafter be sworn and enrolled of that band that is not of tall personage, strong, active and of manlie presence...'

The Yeomen still carry out similar duties on the occasion of State visits, State banquets, the annual Diplomatic Reception and at the State Opening of Parliament.

Yeoman Francis Kerridge saves King George III from being assassinated by Margaret Nicholson an insane woman, on 2 August 1786. From a contemporary sketch.

Royal Meals

In the sixteenth and seventeenth centuries, the serving and eating of Royal meals was an elaborate ritual, often carried out in public, and the Yeomen played their part. Their first duty was to carry in the dishes, and then, as part of their protective role, to taste the food before it was set before the Sovereign.

A contemporary account by Paul Hentzner of Court life under Queen Elizabeth describes her dining in state at Greenwich in 1598:

'The Yeomen of the Guard entered bareheaded, clothed in scarlet, with golden roses upon their backs, bringing in at each turn a course of twenty-four dishes, served in plate, most of them gilt; these dishes were received by gentlemen in the same order they were brought and placed upon the table, while the lady-taster gave to each of the Guard a mouthful to eat of the particular dish he had brought, for fear of poison. During the time that this guard, which consists of the tallest and stoutest men that can be found in all England, being carefully selected for this service, were bringing dinner, twelve trumpets and two kettle-drums made the hall ring...'

Lining the Approaches in 1882. Yeomen on duty at the Royal wedding of Victoria's youngest son, Leopold, Duke of Albany. From a contemporary sketch.

The Yeomen were also present at the banquet held annually in Windsor Castle after the Installation of Knights of the Garter. The Sovereign was served by Gentlemen at Arms, while the Yeomen attended on the Knights, a custom that was discontinued during the time of King George III.

The Banquet in St George's Hall, Windsor, attended by the King and the Knights of the Garter. The Yeomen of the Guard are in the foreground. From an engraving by Hollar, 1672.

Making the Royal Bed

An important part of protecting the Monarch was to ensure that he (or she) slept safe and sound. Assassins might well lurk in the Royal bedroom, or else might leave under the mattress an up-pointed dagger or some other lethal device such as a caltrop (a round metal ball with long sharp spikes, usually employed in battle to throw under the hooves of enemy horses). One was found under the bed of King Henry IV once at Windsor Castle, so the 'making of the Royal Bed' did have some significance as a security measure.

Many of the Royal Household were involved in the ritual and the Yeomen of the Guard played a prominent part. We have a fascinating, first-hand account of the ceremony as it was in the time of Henry VII from an original MS which belonged to the Earl Marshal and contained the whole duty of the Lord Chamberlain, copied out for the instruction of Alan, Earl of Arundel, Lord Chamberlain to King Henry VIII in 1526:

'After bringing in "the stuff for the bed" then the Esquire or the Gentleman Usher shall command them what they shall do. So, first one of them to fetch [test] the straw with a dagger or otherwise (that there be no untruth therein), and then the Yeoman to take the straw and lay it plain and draw down the canvas over it straight. Then shall they lay on the bed of down and one of the Yeomen to tumble up and down upon the same for the search thereof...'

The account goes on to set out in great detail every stage of the bed-making such as placing the sheets, pillow, covers and curtains '... as shall best please the King ...' The task being completed, the orders finish with the very sensible note:

'Item. A groom or page ought to take a torch while the bed is making, and fetch a loaf of bread, a pot of ale, and another of wine, and bring it without the traverse, where all they which were at the making of the bed shall go and drink together.'

The Yeomen of his Majesty's Chamber, as they were called, also travelled round with the Sovereign, like the Body Guard, and a warrant of November 1617, records a 'payment to be made unto Wm. Hawkins, George Turner and John Copping ... for the charges of themselves and their horses in attending on his Majesty's bed, in his progress into Scotland and back, from the 10th of March last until the 22nd of September following, being 198 days, after the rate of 2s.6d. per diem to each of them.'

The Yeomen who actually helped to make the King's bed (and presumably that of the Queen also, although there is no specific evidence on this delicate point) were called *Yeomen Bed-Goers*. Other Yeomen were responsible for looking after the bed and bedding, and all the associated equipment, particularly when the Monarch travelled abroad, and they were known as *Yeomen Bed-Hangers*.

The custom of making the King's bed ceased in the eighteenth century, but these two titles are still granted to senior members of the Body Guard as a special honorary rank, and they carry the letters 'YBG' and 'YBH' after their names in the Nominal Roll of the Guard.

Royal Progresses

Up to the nineteenth century, the Monarch used to make Royal progresses round the kingdom, and the Body Guard not only provided protection and an element of pageantry, but they were also on occasion sent ahead to find suitable accommodation for the Royal party, and to check it and the local populace for any hidden dangers.

The first Royal progress involving the Yeomen was in March 1486, only some six months after they had been formed, when King Henry VII travelled in style to Lincoln and then on to York, with a view to impressing the nobles with his power. The Guard accompanied him throughout, and were a valuable safeguard against possible trouble while in Yorkist territory.

Back Stairs Duty

The Body Guard also carried out until 1775 the intriguing task known as 'back stairs duty'. It was customary before then (and also since) to ensure that all Royal palaces—and also any buildings where meetings were regularly held—had not only a recognised front entrance, but also a private door at the side or back. The

Queen Elizabeth I, with an escort of Yeomen of the Guard, arrives at Nonsuch Palace in Surrey, for a five-days stay with the Earl of Arundel, in 1559. From a picture by Hofnagel.

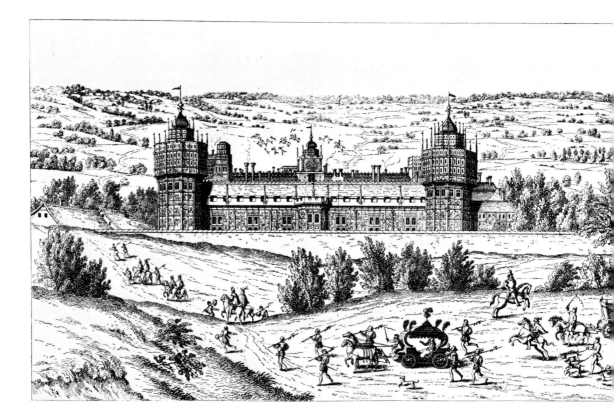

latter was used for all those who were to be admitted unseen to visit the Monarch, be they ministers or mistresses; hence, of course, the phrase 'back stairs influence'.

The responsible duty of receiving and conducting these surreptitious visitors, and keeping out intruders, was carried out by carefully selected, duly discreet Yeomen of the Guard.

The Twentieth Century

In this century the Body Guard have continued their historic role of protecting the Monarch in one way or another through two world wars.

In the 1914–1918 War, the Yeomen were quickly employed as 'Watchers' at Buckingham Palace and Windsor Castle, but within a few months they were replaced by Special Constables. In London the Police Commissioner took great trouble to obtain the right people for this delicate duty, and finally reported with evident satisfaction that the force was 'composed entirely of gentlemen, members of London Clubs and the Bar, all known to each other.'

These very special Specials were evidently a success in the capital looking after the Royal palaces, but at Windsor Castle the Acting Governor declared after a while that he preferred the Yeomen because 'Constables could not take the place of Yeomen of the Guard at Windsor Castle, as the Yeomen formed a trained escort for an anti-aircraft gun mounted there [a naval six-pounder], and that they formed a Guard of 28 men, armed with rifles, ready at a moment's notice to tackle the crew of any airship that might be brought down by gunfire.'

His views were accepted and the Special Constables were withdrawn, though the Chief Constable must have been rather disappointed as he too had been at great pains to recruit them specially—from 'gentlemen of leisure, professional men, and tradesmen of the better class.'

The Acting Governor was to be disappointed too in the end, for he was later told that the Yeomen could no longer be made available, and the task was to be handed over by the War Office to a 'guard of National Reserve Territorials'.

In World War Two the Yeomen were left to play their part as individuals in the national war effort, each according to his own capabilities and inclination. The majority did sterling work in the Home Guard or Civil Defence, but they did it in their own part of the country, rather than being involved in any direct protection of the Sovereign.

Today, as in the past, they remain ready to carry out whatever role is given to them as members of the Queen's Body Guard.

5

Yeomen in Battle

The Yeomen of the Guard won their spurs on the battlefield of Bosworth in 1485, and established themselves there as valiant, reliable fighting men. They were not professional soldiers, but more of an armed bodyguard who were trained and ready to fight as and when required. For the next 280 years they would fight for their Royal master on many occasions, at home and abroad, on land and at sea.

Henry VII

Henry VII had not been two years on the throne before he had to face the first threat to his position. It came from the Earl of Lincoln, an ambitious Lancastrian, who raised the standard of rebellion, and put forward Lambert Simnel as a claimant to the throne.

The King met the rebels on the Field of Stoke on 16 June 1487, and, after a fierce and bloody battle in which there were 6,000 casualties, defeated them. The Body Guard fought alongside the King, and duly justified their new title.

Much the same happened again nine years later when a Fleming, Peter Osbeck, who claimed to be the son of Edward IV, landed in Cornwall and with a number of supporters marched on London. The King, escorted as usual by the Body Guard, met and defeated this pretender at Blackheath on 22 June 1497. Perkin Warbeck, as he is better known to us, was locked up in the Tower, where he was closely guarded by four Yeomen of the Guard, whose orders were that they 'should not the breadth of a nayl go from his person'.

Henry VII had also to compete with the growing power of France, and when Parliament was summoned on 26 January 1492 to consider the problem, he made such a stirring speech, recalling the glories of Crecy, Poitiers and Agincourt, that war was duly declared against France to protect the interests of England. The King then set out at the head of a large army—which included his Yeomen—and besieged Boulogne. It fell within a month, peace was signed and Henry returned with a large indemnity—a brisk, successful campaign by any reckoning.

A hero of this expedition was one of the Yeomen of the Guard, named John Person, 'which was sometimes a baker of Coventry.

Which John Person, after a gun had borne away his foot by the small of the leg, yet that notwithstanding, what setting and what kneeling, shot after many of his arrows, and when the Frenchmen fled, and his fellows were in the chase, he cried to one of his fellows, and said, "Have thou these 6 arrows that I have left and follow thou the chase, for I may not." The which John Person died within a few days after, on whose soul God have mercy.' Had the Victoria Cross then been in existence he must surely have qualified.

Henry VIII

Yeomen of the Guard in their green and white uniform, c 1527, based on a sketch in the illuminated treaty between Henry VIII and Francis I.

The Body Guard saw much action on both land and sea under King Henry VIII. In 1513 he declared war on Francis I of France, and an expedition was mobilised to invade the Continent. Call-up papers were sent to all those who owed service to the Crown, and 'John Randall, Yeoman of the Crown, dwelling in Kent,' for example, was ordered 'to repair to the King's presence to do him service of war over sea.'

The first troops set out in May, and on 20 June, Henry himself sailed across to Calais and took command of his army. He was accompanied by a great retinue and six hundred of his Guard 'all in white gaberdines and cappes'.

Also with the King on this campaign were his other bodyguard, the Band of Gentlemen Spears, which he had created in 1509. Both now escorted the King to battle, and would at the end of the campaign emerge with their first official battle honour.

On 16 August 1513, when the French were defeated at what became known as the Battle of the Spurs, the Yeomen took part, but not unfortunately with their Captain, Sir Henry Marney, as he had earlier had his leg badly broken by a kick from a horse.

Henry now turned his attention to the capture of the city of Tournai: within a few days he had forced it to surrender, and on 24 September he made a triumphal entry, escorted by his Guard in their 'white and green plagards'. He also knighted on this occasion one Anthony Wingfield, who was to become Captain of the Guard in 1539. TOURNAI 1514 is the first battle honour of the Body Guard and appears as such on their Standard.[10]

The King returned to England soon after, but left behind some 300 of his Guard as part of the garrison of Tournai. They remained there until peace was signed in 1519, and it does not seem to have been a particularly popular duty. There were riots over the conditions there and the troops did not receive their pay regularly; the

[10]The date '1514' refers to the time they formed the garrison, rather than to the actual battle in 1513.

A distinguished and famous Yeoman of the Guard, Cornelius Vandun (1483–1577). From an eighteenth-century engraving of his monument in St Margaret's, Westminster. The monument is now very worn and details of dress are indistinguishable.

CORNELIUS VANDUN BORN AT BREDA, SOLDIER
WITH KING HENRY AT TURNEY, YEOMAN OF THE
GUARD, AND USHER TO KING HENRY, KING EDWARD,
QUEEN MARY, AND QUEEN ELIZABETH.
OBIIT 1577 ÆTATIS SUÆ 94.

discipline of the Yeomen of the Guard seems to have been better than most, and when in 1515 '... there happened such a ryot that the citie was in great jeopardy ... all the souldiers except such as were of the kynges garde rebelled, and put the Lord Montjoye [the Governor] in jeopardy of his life.'

When Tournai was given up, 'The King sent for all the Yeomen of the Garde that were come from Tournai, and after many good wordes given to them, he granted them fourpence the day without attendance, except they were specially commanded.'

One of the veteran Yeomen of Tournai may well have been Thomas Hawkins, who lived to be one hundred and one. He was buried at Boughton under Blean in Kent, and on his tombstone was inscribed a verse, some lines of which were:

46

King Henry the Eighth I serv'd, who won me fame,
Which was to me a gracious Prince allwaies,
And made me well to spend my aged daies.
My stature high, my body hugge and strong,
Excelling all that lived in mine age.

The Body Guard were also present at the siege and capture of Boulogne in 1544, but this time they were not left there as part of the garrison. This action is of interest in that the Yeomen fought, for the last time, as part of the army as well as being the King's bodyguard. Certainly they were with King Henry VIII when he personally led the final assault against the town, which resulted in the French agreeing to surrender, provided that they could march out 'with bag and baggage'. This campaign BOULOGNE 1544 is the Yeomen's second battle honour that appears on their Standard.

King Henry VIII at Portsmouth on 29 July 1545, when his flagship The Mary Rose sank before his eyes. From a painting in Cowdray Castle, now destroyed.

Service at Sea. The French were not however finished, and the following year they assembled a great fleet of over 200 ships to invade England. The King promptly concentrated his own forces at Portsmouth and moved there himself, ready to repel the attack. On 29 July 1545, he watched his fleet sail out from the Solent to

47

engage the French, and saw his own flag-ship, the *Mary Rose*, go down with all hands without a shot being fired.

Some of the Body Guard were with the King as he watched events from Southsea Castle, while others were undoubtedly aboard the *Mary Rose*.

Among the 17,000 artefacts brought up from the ship during 1981–1982 were some archers' arm-braces, which may well have belonged to Yeomen of the Guard, particularly as they bear the Royal arms.

It may seem surprising that there were Yeomen of the Guard on board a naval ship, but they could easily have been there in two roles. First, being a Royal bodyguard, they escorted the Sovereign at all times, and this included the occasions on which he went to sea, when they carried out much the same duties as do the Royal Marines today. Second, they were, at times, sent to serve as fighting men with the Navy. Their role then was as archers, acting in much the same way as would the sharpshooters in the rigging at Trafalgar.

When a fleet was being fitted out in 1512 for the impending war against France, the Captain of the Guard, Sir Henry Guilford, was actually appointed captain of a naval ship, the *Sovereign*, and with him were put 'sixty of the tallest Yeomen of the Kynge's Garde'. On 15 August they were in action at sea, and had a narrow escape from destruction when two ships blew up only moments after they had been alongside the *Sovereign*.

It was evidently recognised that service at sea was bound to be a hardship for the Guard, for the Yeomen were duly rewarded with an extra *2d* a day.

Elizabeth I

Since the Queen did not herself lead her army into battle, the Body Guard saw no active service in this reign. The Yeomen were, however, with her when she rode 'clothed in a steel corslet' to Tilbury on 5 August 1588, and made her stirring speech to her troops when the threat from the Spanish Armada was at its height. This scene was lyrically described by a contemporary poet, who even included a reference to the Yeomen:

> *Then came the Queen, on prancing steed*
> *Attired like an angel bright.*
> *And eight brave footmen at her feet,*
> *Whose jerkins were most rich in sight.*
> *Her ladies likewise of great honour*
> *Did sumptuously wait upon her,*
> *With pearls and diamonds brave adorned*

A Yeoman of the Guard from the time of Queen Mary.

Mounted Yeomen of the Guard with Sir Henry Sidney, Viceroy of Ireland, on a visit to Dublin, c 1578. Sir Henry Sidney is preceded by two trumpeters, two Yeomen, a herald, a mace bearer and a sword bearer. From a contemporary illustration.

> *And in caustly cauls of gold.*
> *Her Guard in scarlet then rode after*
> *With bows and arrows stout and bold.*

The Stuarts

Under the Stuarts, the Yeomen of the Guard were regarded as a military body, and were involved in battle on several occasions.

James I laid down what he regarded as the essential requirements for membership of his Guard:

> '... *such men to be recommended unto me for that service as are well known to be of honest conversation, and withall able and active men ... for I hold it fitting to have such a select Guard of able bodyes as may match any other men for their number, in all manly exercises whatsoever ... so that withall they will be well shapt and comely personages, and amongst them to have some that have been either Lieutenants, Ancients [Ensigns] or Sergeants in the warres, I specially allow of.*'[11]

Although James I set great store by having his Guard well trained and ready for war, they did not see action during his reign. It was a very different story under Charles I, when the Guard had to protect the King and the Queen through all the strife of the Civil War of 1642–1649. The Captain at this time was George Goring, Earl of Norwich, who supported the King to the end, and used his Guard to escort him in many battles and moments of danger. They

[11]Orders for the Household of the Prince of Wales, 16 October 1610.

49

were drilled in 'horsemanship' and in 'sword-and-pistol exercises', and were regularly trained in the use of their muskets.

When the young Prince Charles fled to the Continent, the Earl of Norwich and a number of Yeomen went with him and shared his exile, returning with him in triumph on his Restoration as Charles II in 1660. They in fact preceded the King back to England, and the Captain set about re-creating the former Body Guard as far as possible; indeed so successful was he in this, that the Yeomen of the Guard formed part of the Royal procession when it entered the City of London on 20 May 1660.

Once restored to the throne, Charles II brought the Guard up to a strength of 200, and the valiant Lord Norwich, now aged 80, was allowed to retire.

Charles II quickly reorganised the Guard to make it an efficient fighting force, able to play its part alongside his new Standing Army. But they were not in fact involved in battle during his reign or that of his brother James II.

Under William III they did, however, see plenty of active service, accompanying the King on a series of campaigns against France. They also went with him to Ireland in 1690, and took part in the great victory of the Battle of the Boyne, as well as the siege and capture of Limerick.

They must have distinguished themselves on this occasion, for the King decided to take a specially selected detachment with him on his series of campaigns in the Netherlands from 1691 to 1701. This detachment must have been mounted, for a Royal warrant of 8 April 1691 records that they were each issued with a carbine, a bucket and a cartouche box. The King was himself usually in the thick of the fighting, being wounded three times, for example, at the Battle of Neerwinden in 1693. No doubt there were casualties too among the Yeomen, who must have had a difficult and anxious time trying to protect him.

The House of Hanover

The final act in the Body Guard's duty of protecting the Sovereign in battle came on 27 June 1743 at the Battle of Dettingen, when King George II personally commanded the British Army at that victory against the French. It was the last time that a reigning King of England led his troops into battle, and as Colonel Hennell remarks in his history of the Guard, 'With the death of their fighting King [in 1760] the Guard laid aside for ever their duties as soldiers in the field.'

This was not the end however of 'Yeomen in Battle', for from 1830 King William IV, strongly supported by the Duke of Wellington, filled the ranks of the Guard with veterans of both the

Peninsular Campaign and Waterloo, in place of the civilians who had found their way into the Guard during the previous 70 years. So the Yeomen retained their honourable status as fighting men, and it has remained that way ever since.

The standard was set by the first veteran to become a Yeoman under the new system. He was Sergeant-Major Thomas Baker of the Coldstream Guards, who joined the Body Guard in 1823, having been appointed specifically as a reward for distinguished service. His record was certainly impressive, for having enlisted in 1799, he saw action in Cadiz (1800), Egypt (1801), Germany (1805), and Copenhagen (1807); he also fought in the Peninsular Campaign from 1811 to 1814, and was then at Waterloo.

In 1832, thanks to the new rules, he was joined by three more veterans, Corporal-of-Horse Charles Baker of The First Life Guards, and Farrier-Major Thomas Lea and Corporal-of-Horse Benjamin Blackey, both from The Royal Horse Guards. Two years later another new Yeoman was Sergeant-Major Thomas Dudley, 14th Light Dragoons who had no less than 11 clasps to his Peninsular Medal.

So it has been ever since, with the Body Guard being composed of the best elements from the Army and the Royal Marines. After World War Two members of the Royal Air Force became eligible, and the first one, Flight-Sergeant Hewlett, joined in 1955. Today, every Yeoman must have served his country with distinction, as was evident in 1979 when 81 Yeomen mustered between them no less than 540 awards for gallantry and campaign medals.

Nor have the Yeomen ever been content to remain in retirement when needed by their country. On the outbreak of World War One the entire Body Guard volunteered for active service and was duly placed at the disposal of the War Office for the training of a younger generation. Some of them did manage to see active service and fought in Flanders and elsewhere overseas. Some rose to commissioned rank, though they had to relinquish this at the end of the war if they wanted to become Yeomen of the Guard again.

Much the same occurred in World War Two. Those Yeomen who were fit enough re-joined their regiments and proved invaluable as instructors, while, as mentioned, others played their part in the Home Guard or Civil Defence.

Those joining the Body Guard since 1945 have seen service in many areas round the world, ranging from Korea and Malaya to Aden, Burma and Ulster. Their ranks include not only infantrymen, but also paratroops, commandos, pilots and even the Special Air Service. There is no doubt that the Yeomen of today have much in common, when it comes to battle, with those stalwart Yeomen on the battlefield of Bosworth.

6

Ceremonial Duties

'For the maintenance and upholding of the dignity and grandeur of the English Crown, in perpetuity, his successors, the Kings and Queens of England for all time.'

Thus did Henry VII define the role of the Yeomen of his Guard, and there can be no doubt that they have lived up to his expectations. For five centuries they have been present at virtually every Royal State occasion in England and Wales, not only in their traditional role as a Royal bodyguard, but also as part of the ceremonial associated with the Monarchy. As such, they are an essential part of the pageantry of our country.

Coronations

From the Coronation of King Henry VII onwards the Yeomen have played a part in this impressive ceremony. They are in attendance on the Monarch in Westminster Abbey, and also at Buckingham Palace. In addition they provide four 'wheelmen', who walk in the royal procession beside the State coach 'in line with and three paces from the front and rear axles.'

A coronation is, today, one of the few occasions on which 'wheelmen' are required, the criterion being that the procession must be going at a walking pace, rather than a trot. There used to be 'wheelmen' at the State Opening of Parliament, but not after it was decreed that the Royal procession should 'break into a trot'.

Funerals

Until the death of Queen Victoria in 1901 the Yeomen of the Guard had the privilege (except for the period 1509–1684) of carrying the Sovereign's coffin at the funeral. They bore the body of their founder, King Henry VII, to his tomb in Westminster Abbey, but when Henry VIII died in 1547 this honour was claimed by the Gentlemen of the Privy Chamber, and they continued to carry out the duty until 1684 when Charles II died. During this period, the Yeomen had to be content with marching in the funeral procession.

Officers and Yeomen of the Guard in a Coronation procession, date uncertain.

Yeomen marching alongside the State coach as 'wheelmen' at the State Opening of Parliament on 6 February, 1911, the first Parliament to be opened by the new king, George V.

Evelyn records in his diary that Charles II 'was obscurely buried at night, in a vault under Henry VII's Chapel in Westminster, without great pomp'. But from then on for the next 150 years the Yeomen once more had the privilege of carrying the coffin. The reason why they resumed this particular duty is uncertain, though Thomas Preston has suggested that 'the coffin was found to be too heavy for the Gentlemen [of the Privy Chamber] and required men of more robust habit.'

Whatever the reason why the Gentlemen abandoned the task, the Yeomen gladly took on the duty again, which meant that they played a major role at Royal funerals. They guarded the Sovereign's body, took part in the Lying-in-State, and then marched in the funeral procession in their traditional place at the end.

Yeomen, as wheelmen, escorting the State coach around the Queen Victoria memorial outside Buckingham Palace in the Coronation Procession of King George VI, 27 May 1937.

Yeomen with the State coach at the Coronation Procession of Queen Elizabeth II, 2 June 1953.

Yeomen with partisans reversed on duty at the Lying-in-State of King Edward VII in 1910. Next to the catafalque are the Gentlemen at Arms in their role as 'The Nearest Guard'.

Yeomen marching, with partisans reversed, in the funeral procession of King Edward VII, 1910; the new king, George V can be seen in his uniform of Admiral of the Fleet.

Finally, twelve Yeomen carried the coffin on its last journey to the graveside.

On the occasion of Royal funerals the Yeomen have always worn a black cloak or 'caule' which completely covers their uniform; they continue this tradition today.

At the funeral of William IV in 1837 they kept a vigil over the coffin at the Lying-in-State in Windsor Castle, and also lined the entrances to the room where it lay. They then provided the customary bearer party of twelve Yeomen for the final rites in St George's Chapel. But this was to be the last time.

Queen Victoria requested in her will that she might receive the simple funeral of a soldier's daughter. It was therefore decided by King Edward VII, when she died in 1901, that the coffin should be carried, not by Yeomen of the Guard, but by the Queen's Company of the Grenadier Guards, so as to avoid any suggestion that the funeral was being made a State occasion, contrary to the Queen's wishes.

So it was that the Grenadier Guards escorted Queen Victoria's coffin on its sad journey from Osborne, through the capital and on to Windsor; and they have carried out this duty ever since.

The Monarch used, in olden times, to lie in state wherever he or she died. Henry VIII, for example, lay at Whitehall Palace, and George III at Windsor Castle, but since 1910 the formal Lying-in-State has been at Westminster Hall, followed by a funeral procession through London and burial at Windsor.

Normally, the Body Guard only attend the Lying-in-State of the Sovereign, but in 1861, as a special tribute to the Duke of Wellington, Queen Victoria authorised the presence of the Yeomen of the Guard at his Lying-in-State. They did not, however, take part in the vigil for Sir Winston Churchill in 1965, although they were in the funeral procession.

State Visits Abroad

The Yeomen of the Guard no longer accompany the Sovereign on State visits abroad, but in Tudor times they were very much a part of the Royal Household on these occasions, and they played a significant part in the maintenance and upholding of the dignity and grandeur of the English Crown.

Yeomen of the Guard are among those escorting King Henry VIII at his meeting with Emperor Maximilian. From carvings on the Emperor's tomb in Innsbruck in Austria.

This was never more so than when Henry VIII indulged in the historic extravaganza known as The Field of Cloth of Gold in June 1520. When a treaty was concluded with the French in 1519, Henry decided that the meeting needed to ratify the treaty should be an occasion for all the pomp and circumstance he could arrange. The French accepted his implicit challenge, and each monarch set about trying to outdo the other.

Planning and preparations took a year and 5,000 workmen were employed to build the setting. Cardinal Wolsey represented the King in choosing the Val d'Or, as a neutral site astride the boundary between English and French territory in Normandy. Ten thousand locals were removed from the area, and a vast elaborate camp was set up.

The Royal retinue that set out from Dover on 31 May 1520 totalled 3,997 people and 2,087 horses. Among them were 200 Yeomen of the Guard who had been selected as being the 'tallest and most erect persons'.

A fine picture at Hampton Court, attributed to Hans Holbein, shows the scene in all its magnificence as the English Royal cavalcade approaches the meeting place of the two Monarchs.

Mounted Yeomen, with their bows, escorting King Henry VIII at his meeting with Francis I of France at the Field of Cloth of Gold, 1520. From a bas-relief at Rouen in France.

Henry VIII rides a white courser and is surrounded by Yeomen of the Guard on foot, with partisans on their shoulders and dressed in scarlet. Other Yeomen guard the camp entrance, together with French soldiers in their blue and yellow uniforms.

In the background one can see the bakeries and kitchens preparing for the great banquets, and a further party of Yeomen carrying out their other duty of serving the food at the King's table. Fourteen of them, each bearing a covered dish, can be seen going towards the Royal pavilion, led by the Lord Steward with his white wand of office.

The festivities continued for over three weeks, from the 4th to the 28th of June, with jousting, feasting and dancing, as well as endless contests between the English and the French, each Monarch being determined to score over the other wherever possible. The Yeomen were called upon to play their part, not only in the pageantry and ceremonial, but also by competing in archery and wrestling, at both of which they excelled.

The Field of Cloth of Gold was, sadly, the last official State visit abroad on which the Sovereign took his Yeomen with him, and today they do not normally accompany the Monarch on overseas

tours. They have, however, been present on State visits to Scotland and Ireland.

In 1633, King Charles I travelled to Edinburgh and was crowned there on 18 May; he was accompanied by a detachment of the Yeomen of the Guard, though the Scots claimed the right to protect him within their own Kingdom.

The only other State visit to Scotland was in 1823, when King George IV sailed to Leith in the Royal yacht *The Royal George*. He took with him 16 of the Body Guard, who took part in the Royal procession, but not as 'the Nearest Guard', this honour having been granted for the first time to the Royal Company of Archers.

This body, dating back to 1676, was some 400 strong, and composed of the nobility and gentry of Scotland; they petitioned the King in 1822 that they might be allowed to act as his bodyguard during his forthcoming visit to Scotland. This was agreed and they were duly appointed as 'The Sovereign's Body Guard of Scotland', a position that is now firmly established. They wear a uniform of field green, with a be-feathered bonnet and a longbow and they act as the Nearest Guard to the Sovereign on State occasions north of the border.

Although the Yeomen of the Guard ceased to do duty in Scotland, they did travel to Dublin with King George V on his State visit there in 1911, and to Belfast with Queen Elizabeth II for her Silver Jubilee visit in 1977.

Earlier in their history they had spent many years in Ireland as the bodyguard of the Sovereign's representative there, the Viceroy and later the Lord Lieutenant. In 1520, for example, Henry VIII appointed the Earl of Surrey to this post and set him up with a miniature Court, which included 400 Yeomen, though this was soon reduced to 300. They received 6*d* a day extra pay, but it seems to have been an unpopular duty, and many of them applied to return home, even though it meant leaving the Body Guard.

Towards the end of the seventeenth century—possibly in 1684—a new body was created in Ireland called the Battle-Axe Guard. This was modelled on the Yeomen of the Guard, and it may even have included some former Yeomen; certainly they took over from the Yeomen of the Guard their role of attendance on the Lord Lieutenant of Ireland on State occasions. The earliest Royal warrant concerning them is dated 30 October 1704; and they consisted then of a Captain, two Lieutenants, two Sergeants and 50 Yeomen.[12]

The Battle-Axe Guard was disbanded in 1833, due to economies

[12] An account of the guard was written by Sir Bernard Burke, taken from the records at the Office of Arms, Dublin Castle.

in the vice-regal budget, and has never been revived. Their home was in Dublin Castle, and the Battle-Axe Hall there is still sometimes referred to as 'Beefeater Hall', thus linking this term with Royal bodyguards in general.

State Visits at Home

Throughout their history the Yeomen of the Guard have formed part of the pomp and pageantry with which Kings and Queens of England have welcomed distinguished visitors to this country. In 1506, for example, Henry VII sent a detachment to meet Philip of Castile, after he had been shipwrecked near Weymouth, and they then escorted him to Windsor.

State visits along the lines that we know today did not begin until the nineteenth century, the first one being the gathering of sovereigns of the Grand Alliance in 1814 after the exile of Napoleon Bonaparte. They grew in frequency during Queen Victoria's reign, and today there are usually two a year, one in the Spring and one in the Autumn.

Yeomen of the Guard escort Marie de Medici, on a visit to her daughter Queen Henrietta Maria, past Cheapside Cross on her visit to England in 1638. From a contemporary print.

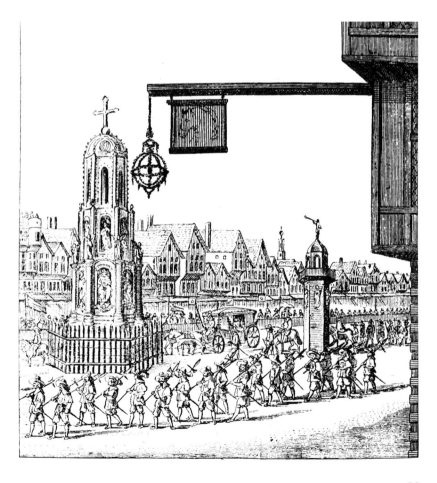

Yeomen on duty during the State visit to Britain of Emperor Napoleon III in 1855; Britain and France were united as allies in the Crimean War.

Queen Victoria receives Emperor Napoleon III at Windsor.

When a visiting head of state arrives at Buckingham Palace or Windsor Castle, the entrance and the corridors are lined by both the Gentlemen at Arms and the Yeomen of the Guard, each with their Standard.

The occasion normally includes a State banquet either in the Ball Room at Buckingham Palace or in St George's Hall at Windsor Castle, and this is attended by the Body Guard but not the Gentlemen at Arms. A detachment of two Sergeant-Majors and 20 Yeomen, commanded by an Exon, line the entrance to the Banqueting Hall, and also stand guard during the meal, with the Exon positioned immediately behind the Sovereign. It is a long and tantalising duty for, while the distinguished guests tuck into the banquet, the Yeomen can only stand and wait, thinking perhaps of the time when their predecessors not only carried the dishes for the Royal table, but also 'tasted' them.

They are, however, given a meal and a welcome drink afterwards at the Palace. If the banquet is at Windsor Castle, they are returned to London in a comfortable bus, as opposed to the last century when they had to travel by train and then sleep in the corridors of St James's Palace for what remained of the night.

The Exon, too, has a meal provided after the banquet, which is something to think of while he stands on duty. An Exon at the beginning of this century recalled one State banquet at which King Alfonso of Spain, in whose honour it was being held, came up to him afterwards and said he 'hoped I was not as hungry as I looked'.

State Opening of Parliament

The State Opening of Parliament by the Sovereign is one of the most historic and symbolic of our national ceremonial occasions,

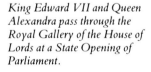

King Edward VII and Queen Alexandra pass through the Royal Gallery of the House of Lords at a State Opening of Parliament.

Yeomen of the Guard line the Grand Staircase at Buckingham Palace in 1851, as Queen Victoria leaves the Palace to open Parliament.

Yeomen escort Queen Victoria from Buckingham Palace to the State Opening of Parliament, 1851.

for it relates back to the very beginning of the British Monarchy and the constitution. The Body Guard are closely involved, not only in the ceremonial, but also in the traditional 'Search' of the cellars, described in detail in the next chapter.

The Captain of the Guard and the Lieutenant both form part of the Royal procession, positioned alongside their counterparts in the Gentlemen at Arms, who, being the Nearest Guard, are on the right.

The Clerk of the Cheque, the Ensign and one Exon form up with 24 Yeomen and line the Royal Gallery through which the Royal procession passes into the House of Lords.

It can be an awkward moment for the Ensign, as the many distinguished guests standing close behind him on this occasion are liable to be prodded in the stomach as he lowers the Standard to the Queen as she passes!

Yeomen line the Royal Staircase, Victoria Tower at Westminster as Queen Victoria arrives for the State Opening of Parliament, 1851.

Investiture of the Prince of Wales

The ceremonial Investiture of the Prince of Wales is one of those moments of pageantry that has been revived during this century. Prior to that it took place at Westminster with remarkably little ceremonial. But when Prince Edward (later King Edward VIII)

The Investiture of the Prince of Wales (later King Edward VIII) at Caernarvon Castle, 13 July, 1911. The Prince is accompanied by his mother, Queen Mary.

Yeomen of the Guard 'off duty' at the Investiture of the Prince of Wales, 1911.

8 The Royal Procession in St
Paul's Cathedral on St George's
Day 1789, at the Thanksgiving
Service called to celebrate the
King's 'happy recovery'. The
Yeomen line both sides of the
aisle through which the Royal
party passes. From an engraving
by J Neagle after a drawing by
E Dayes 'draughtsman to the
Duke of York'.

9 George Colman, Esquire, the
Lieutenant of the Yeomen of the
Guard, in the extravagant
Tudor-style uniform ordered to
be worn by George IV for his
Coronation in 1821.

10 Reception at the Great West Door of St Paul's Cathedral before the Jubilee Service in 1935
for King George V and Queen Mary. The Yeomens' uniforms are shown in perfect detail.
Painting by Frank Salisbury.

11 The marriage of the Prince of Wales (later King Edward VII) to Princess Alexan[...]
Denmark in 1863. Two Yeomen stand guard by a door to one side of the altar.

12 Yeomen, in black caules with their partisans reversed, stand at the four corners of the catafalque during the Lying-in-State of King George V at Westminster Hall, 1936. Painting by Frank Beresford.

13 Detail from the Lying-in-State of George V. Yeomen always attend the Lying-in-State of the Monarch. They used to carry the coffin as well, until Queen Victoria announced that she wished for the 'simple funeral of a soldier's daughter' and, as a result, her coffin was carried by the Grenadier Guards who have continued this duty ever since.

14 Yeomen stand guard as the Queen presents her son Charles, Prince of Wales, to the people at the King's Gate of Caernarvon Castle, 1 July 1969.

15 The Queen turns and surveys the scene from the steps of St Paul's Cathedral as she arrives for her Silver Jubilee Thanksgiving Service 7 June 1977. The Yeomen acting as 'wheelmen' stand on either side of the Gold State coach.

16 Flanked by Yeomen, Ronald Reagan, as President of the United States, addresses members of both Houses of Parliament in the Royal Gallery of the Palace of Westminster.

17 The Queen surrounded by members of her Body Guard for an official group photograph taken in the grounds of Buckingham Palace following their annual inspection.

was due to be invested, that fervent Welshman David Lloyd-George, who was Prime Minister at the time, persuaded the King not only to revive the full ceremonial but also to hold the event in Wales at Caernarvon Castle.

So on 13 July 1911, the Investiture took place as a great Welsh occasion, and the Body Guard, with their strong Welsh connections,[13] were proud to play their part.

The second Investiture took place in 1969, when Prince Charles took his title, and again the Yeomen of the Guard were there.

The Garter Service

The Yeomen of the Guard have long been associated with the ancient ceremony at Windsor Castle when the Knights of the Most Noble Order of the Garter hold their annual chapter meeting and service there. The Sovereign is present as head of the order, and the Body Guard parade in attendance on her. They also attend Investitures for other Orders of Chivalry when the Sovereign is present.

The Garter, the senior Order of Chivalry, pre-dates even the Yeomen of the Guard, having been created by King Edward III in 1348. It was originally formed as a brotherhood of 26 Christian Knights, headed by the King and the Prince of Wales. The Order usually met at Windsor once a year and the gathering used to be on St George's Day (23 April); there would be jousting and feasting as well as a service in St George's Chapel. Now they meet in mid-June, usually on the Monday of Royal Ascot week, and hold their Chapter in Windsor Castle in the morning, when any new Knights are invested with due ceremony. There is then a lunch in the Castle, followed by a procession to St George's Chapel for a service.

The Yeomen have, since Tudor times, formed part of the Garter procession, one of the most impressive scenes of pageantry, representing, as it does, the history of England over six centuries.

The route is lined by both Household Cavalry and Foot Guards, and the procession is led by the Constable and Governor of Windsor Castle. Behind come the Military Knights of Windsor, in their unique uniform of a scarlet swallow-tail coat, a white, crossed sword-belt and cocked hat. They are closely linked to the Order of the Garter, in that they were appointed by Edward III as part of the Order, with the task of representing the Knights at the daily Mass that was required of them, but which it was not always possible for them to celebrate at Windsor in person. The Military Knights were originally, and still are 'deserving veteran knights',

---

[13] In Tudor times they received a special Royal grant to celebrate St David's Day with a 'feaste'.

being former Army officers who are given apartments in Windsor Castle as a place of retirement.

Next come the Heralds, followed by the Knights of the Garter themselves, and immediately behind the Sovereign march the officers and Yeomen of the Guard in their traditional place at the rear of the procession. Once inside the Chapel, they remain on guard inside the door until the end of the service, when they form up at the bottom of the steps to salute the Queen as she departs.

Yeomen of the Guard in attendance on King George V at the Bath Service at Westminster Abbey, 1928.

7

Special Body Guard Occasions

There are certain occasions during the year, ceremonial and other, in which the Yeomen of the Guard take part and which are peculiar to them. They are, in their order of occurrence:

> *The Epiphany Service*
> *The Maundy Service*
> *The Inspection of the Body Guard*
> *The Roger Monk Dinner*
> *The Search*
> *Anniversaries*

The Epiphany Service

The Yeomen of the Guard play a special part in the Epiphany Service, which is held in the Chapel Royal at St James's Palace every year on the twelfth day after Christmas.

This very ancient ceremony has been celebrated by the Christian Church since its foundation, to honour the Three Wise Men who travelled to Bethlehem, bringing gifts of gold, frankincense and myrrh to the infant Jesus in his stall. The occasion is celebrated with particular solemnity at the Chapel Royal, because the Sovereign used personally to present gold, frankincense and myrrh to the Church at Epiphany as a Royal offering. This ceased in the time of George III, but the ceremony continues, and today the Sovereign is represented by two Gentlemen Ushers, escorted by a detachment of Yeomen of the Guard.

It is an impressive scene. On the altar is the Chapel's magnificent seventeenth century sacramental plate. The choir, who have the title 'The Gentlemen and Children of the Chapel Royal', are in Royal scarlet, embroidered with gold, while in the aisle stand ten Yeomen of the Guard in their State dress of scarlet and gold.

The two Gentlemen Ushers chosen to represent the Sovereign wear the full ceremonial uniform of the service to which they belong, for they are all former officers in the Armed Forces. As the moment comes during the service for the presentation of the offerings, they advance together to the altar, followed by an escort of a Sergeant-Major and two Yeomen of the Guard.

One Gentlemen Usher carries on a silver-gilt tray 25 gold

sovereigns, obtained from the Bank of England specially for the occasion. These are changed afterwards into pound notes, which are then given to charity. The other Usher bears a similar salver on which are frankincense and myrrh.

Three times the Gentlemen Ushers pause in the aisle and bow to the altar, before laying their Royal offerings on the alms dish held by the Sub-Dean, who is also one of the domestic chaplains to the Sovereign. The Yeomen of the Guard stand close behind, and when the Royal offering has been laid upon the altar, they escort them back to their pew.

It is a ceremony full of history, for the service is as old as Christianity, and the Yeomen of the Guard have attended the Sovereign, or the Sovereign's representative, at this alms-giving for as long as they have existed.

The Maundy Service

Another ancient Royal ceremony at which the Yeomen of the Guard are always in attendance is the Maundy Service held every year on the Thursday before Easter. On this occasion the Sovereign distributes 'Royal Maundy', which consists of specially minted coins given to as many men and as many women as the Sovereign's age in years.

The custom of the Monarch in person distributing alms on Maundy Thursday dates back to the twelfth century, and there are records showing that it has taken place every year since the reign of Edward I (1272–1307). It was, in mediaeval times, regarded as an occasion for public Royal humility as well as charity, and Queen Mary walked on her knees washing and kissing the feet of a group of poor people, just as Jesus had done, before giving them gifts, including her own gown. Queen Elizabeth I was somewhat more realistic; she washed and kissed the feet of the poor, but not until they had first been given a preparatory scrub in warm, scented water by the Yeomen of the Laundry. She also decided not to present her gown to one lucky person, but instead to redeem it by a gift of twenty shillings to each of the men and women present.

The Yeomen of the Guard have participated in the Maundy Service ever since they escorted Henry VII to his first Royal Maundy, held at Lincoln in 1486, when 'he washed the feet of 29 poor men and gave them alms'. There is also a contemporary account of Queen Elizabeth attending a Maundy Service at Greenwich in 1572. The custom of washing the feet of the Maundy recipients, in memory of the Last Supper, was discontinued in 1730, but the Lord High Almoner and his assistants are still girded with linen towels at the Maundy ceremony as a reminder of the ancient custom.

Distribution of the Maundy Money in the Banqueting Hall, Whitehall, 1773. Contemporary engraving.

Queen Elizabeth II passes through a guard of honour provided by the Yeomen as she leaves Westminster Abbey after the Maundy Service, 1981.

From about this time the Monarch ceased to attend the Maundy Service in person, but the custom was happily revived 202 years later by King George V. In this reign, Queen Elizabeth II has done much to give greater emphasis to this traditional ceremony. She has not only distributed Royal Maundy personally almost every year of her reign, but has arranged that two years out of three the service is held in a different cathedral or church round the

The Yeomen of the Guard with the Maundy Money at Westminster Abbey.

The Maundy Service at Salisbury Cathedral, 1974.

country, rather than always being at Westminster Abbey, as used to be the practice. The ceremony is thus not only seen and enjoyed by many more people, but those who receive the treasured Maundy money come from all parts of the country; they are no longer chosen from the poor, but from those who have given particularly worthy service to the Church and to the community.

The Yeomen of the Guard play a prominent part in the ceremony, where they are in close attendance on the Sovereign in their traditional role as an 'Indoor Guard'. The detachment on parade consists of a Sergeant-Major and 18 Yeomen, while an officer, usually the Clerk of the Cheque, attends the Sovereign.

Two Yeomen form part of the Royal procession, and they carry over their heads on their flat-topped head dress the large silver-gilt dishes on which are laid out the be-ribboned purses containing the Maundy money.

Most of the procession, but not the Yeomen, traditionally carry nose-gays, which are presented to them at the start of the service. This is an ancient custom dating back to the days when such bouquets were a necessary protection against the odours and infections of a city's insanitary streets.

There are two distributions of Maundy gifts, all made personally by the Sovereign to each recipient. First, each of the women receives a green purse, and each of the men a white purse, containing £3 in lieu of the former gift of clothing.

Then, later in the service, each person receives two more purses, one containing £2.50 and the other the specially minted Maundy coins, which consist of silver pennies, two-penny, three-penny and four-penny pieces, totalling as many pence as the age of the Sovereign in years.[14]

The Maundy service is one of the few occasions when the Yeomen of the Guard can be seen on parade on their own and outside London.

The Search

Towards the end of October 1605, a Roman Catholic peer called Lord Monteagle received an anonymous warning not to attend the State Opening of Parliament which was due to take place on 5 November. Although not very clear, this sounded ominous, so he took the letter to the Earl of Salisbury, Chief of the Council. King James I, who was due to open Parliament in person, was away hunting, but when he was told of the letter, he immediately ordered the Lord Chamberlain to investigate.

Accompanied by Lord Monteagle, the Lord Chamberlain sear-

[14] The coins were changed from 'old' to 'new' pence in 1971 when Britain went decimal.

King George II crossing the Horse Guards Parade on his way to open Parliament in 1754, with Yeomen acting as 'wheelmen' for his coach. Contemporary engraving.

ched the Parliament Chamber, and the vaults and cellars under the House. In one of these they found an immense quantity of wood and coal, and in charge of it was Guy Fawkes. Their suspicions were aroused, but they only enquired to whom it belonged, and were told that it was the property of Guy Fawkes' master, a Mr Percy, who was one of the Gentlemen Pensioners.

This was immediately reported to the King, who ordered that a thorough search be made of the cellars that very night, 4 November, and also of any adjoining houses. This was done by Sir Thomas Knevet, a magistrate of Westminster and a privy councillor, and he actually caught Guy Fawkes just as he was leaving the cellar. The wood and coal were then overturned, and underneath were found 36 barrels of gunpowder, calculated to contain about six tons, enough to destroy the whole of the Houses of Parliament.

They then searched Guy Fawkes and found on him matches, touchwood and a slow fuse. He was placed under close guard, and Sir Thomas hurried off to report to the King at Whitehall Palace. The King was asleep, but when woken ordered that Guy Fawkes should be brought to him immediately. He personally interrogated him, and as a result, ordered Guy Fawkes to be taken to the Tower.

It is not clear whether the Body Guard carried out the search that discovered Guy Fawkes. One report, a State paper, says that Sir Thomas Knevet was 'accompanied by a sufficient number of assistants' while another says 'by a body of soldiers'. The latter would almost certainly have been the Yeomen of the Guard, but it is quite possible that, to avoid attracting undue attention, Sir Thomas may have employed civilians for the search. What is certain is that it was Yeomen of the Guard who held Guy Fawkes immediately after his capture, conducted him the King and then escorted him to the Tower.

Today the famous Gunpowder Plot is still commemorated when a detachment of the Body Guard carries out a ceremonial search of

*The Search Party of the
Yeomen of the Guard parading
before the Opening of
Parliament, 1901. From a
photograph taken by Sir
Benjamin Stone.*

the cellars of the Palace of Westminster before every State Opening
of Parliament, looking for another Guy Fawkes who might mean
harm. Such a search is, sadly, no mere formality in this age of ter-
rorism, and the somewhat anachronistic efforts of the Yeomen of
the Guard are reinforced by a thorough check carried out by the
Police using electronic devices, sniffer dogs and mine detectors.

There was one occasion in 1943 when the Secretary to the Lord
Great Chamberlain took it upon himself to arrange for the Home
Guard to carry out the Search. There were instant protests from
the Yeomen of the Guard, and it was confirmed that this was
'purely a war-time measure', and that there would be 'no interrup-
tion in future of the traditional and time-honoured deployment of
the Yeomen of the Guard' for this ceremony.

It is thought that the Search may have been carried out before
every State Opening since 1605, though there is no written evidence of this until 1760, and then it comes not from any State
documents but, strangely, from the accounts of a wine merchant.
In that year the firm of Bellamy was granted permission to rent and
use as wine cellars some of the empty vaults under the Houses of
Parliament. The founder of the firm, 'Old Bellamy' as he was called,
instituted the custom whereby the Yeomen of the Guard carrying out the Search happened to end up at his wine store. Having
reported that all was well, they were given a glass of Bellamy's port
in which they drank the Loyal Toast, and one to their host.

The Search Party being inspected, 1960.

Right: 'Ready to move off', 1980. Watched by Royal portraits and a statue of the young Queen Victoria, the Yeomen prepare to search the vaults of Parliament.

When the Houses of Parliament were burned down in 1834, Bellamy's cellars were moved to Parliament Street, but the custom was continued, with the Yeomen adjourning there for their traditional drink after they had completed their Search.[15] It later died out, however, but was revived again in 1976 by the Lord Great Chamberlain.

The size of the search party has varied over the years. The Junior Exon seems to have been put in charge, for as long as he has existed and under him there has always been a Sergeant-Major and a number of Yeomen. In 1802 it was four Yeomen, but by 1900 it had risen to ten and is still that number today.

The Search is a fascinating if inevitably somewhat anachronistic

[15] In 1887 the Queen wrote to Bellamy's and thanked them for 'their kind and loyal custom of drinking her Majesty's health'.

Right: The Search, 1967.

ceremony. The Detachment assembles in the Prince's Chamber of the House of Lords, wearing their splendid uniforms, but without their partisans. The Exon reports to the Gentleman Usher of the Black Rod.

'The Queen's Body Guard of the Yeomen of the Guard, Present, Sir.'

Black Rod then replies, 'Captain Exon,[16] please start to search.'

The Yeomen are then issued with small oil lamps, once the only illumination, but now the Sergeant-Major's chief concern is to see that the Yeomen keep them well away from their £1,000 uniforms!

The Exon gives what must be the unique word of command, 'Yeomen, pick up your lamps,' whereupon the party then moves off down narrow winding stairs into the bowels of the building. It is an incongruous procession, led by the Exon, passing along the brilliantly lit passages lined with a maze of air-conditioning and central heating pipes, and signs such as 'Warning. Lining contains

[16] The traditional title for Exons of the Guard.

Asbestos', 'Mind Your Head' and 'This point is 440 volts. Check voltage of your tool.'

Low clearance is a problem. There are hot pipes at the five foot level and most of the Yeomen are all of six foot. One Exon, who stood seven foot in his cocked hat, asked someone to show him a way round one such hazard—and was lost for twenty-five minutes! Several vertical ladders have to be descended, which proves no easy task for burly Yeomen with their swords. They move in a stately file, marching in slow time, watched by incredulous, grinning young technicians manning the boilers and the machinery.

It is hot, dusty and tiring, and the Yeomen find it a relief to return to ground floor level after an hour of somewhat undignified scrambling, there to enjoy their glass of port.

The Search is an ancient custom, and is valued as such by the Yeomen, but it is perhaps a duty that is less justified than most, largely because it is not seen by any but a small and unappreciative audience.

Inspections

Being the personal Body Guard of the Monarch, the Yeomen have been inspected by the Sovereign frequently throughout their history. When they were permanently on duty at Court, there was a daily muster parade, with more detailed inspections for special occasions. Charles I, for example, ordered a thorough inspection of the Body Guard in 1627, and promptly declared that 30 of the Yeomen were unfit for duty by reason of age or infirmity.

In 1837, William IV inspected them at St James's Palace to see how they looked as a result of his ruling that they should be recruited only from former members of the Army and Marines. It is reported that he 'expressed his entire satisfaction'.

When it was decided under the Regency (1811-1820) that the Yeomen should no longer live at Court, new arrangements were called for. The Division on duty were paraded daily for a roll call, but in addition the Captain was also required under the new system to arrange an annual roll call, when all the officers and Yeomen paraded and answered their names. The Captain then reported to the Sovereign that the Body Guard was present and fit for duty.

Up till the 1860s the Yeomen paraded with muskets and used to march past the Captain as inspecting officer; but the few civilians left in the ranks 'not being able to move with the same celerity as the regular Non Commissioned Officers,' the march past was given up, and after 1866 muskets were no longer carried.

This occasion was more a roll call than an inspection, and so it remained until 1875 when the Prince of Wales (the future King Edward VII) carried out a formal inspection. He commented that

The annual roll call of Officers of the Body Guard, 1859. The Ensign is wearing a colour belt, although there was at that time no Standard for him to carry. The Yeomen in the background are parading with muskets, a habit that was continued until the early 1860s.

The Inspection by King Edward VIII of the Body Guard on 26 June 1936.

the Yeomen with beards looked better than the others, and it then became customary for all the Yeomen to wear beards, a practice that continued until 1936 when King George VI declared that beards should be made 'optional'.

From 1875 the Inspection became an annual ceremony of some importance; it took place in the grounds of St James's Palace, as this was close to the headquarters of the Guard, and was carried out by the Captain, a member of the Royal Family or a distinguished General.

Queen Elizabeth II inspects the Body Guard in the garden of Buckingham Palace, 1958. She is escorted by the Earl of Onslow and Major-General Sir Allan Adair.

Below: The Body Guard march past the Queen after their Inspection in 1958. They are led by Lieutenant-Colonel VB Turner, VC, and Messenger Sergeant-Major R Baker.

'Three Cheers for her Majesty'. The Yeomen cheer following their Inspection by the Queen.

In 1891 Kaiser Wilhelm took the Inspection and was so impressed by the Yeomen that he presented them with his portrait; it was duly hung in the Guardroom at St James's Palace, but has not been seen since World War One.

In 1897, the year of her Diamond Jubilee, Queen Victoria inspected the Body Guard and the parade took place for the first time in the grounds of Buckingham Palace.

Now the Muster Parade and Inspection is carried out annually by the Captain at St James's Palace, and every fourth year the Body Guard is inspected by the Monarch in the garden of Buckingham Palace, or if it rains in the Picture Gallery of the Palace itself.

It is an impressive sight with the Yeomen marching on to parade while a Guards Band plays *The Soldiers of the Queen*. The Guard are then drawn up in their four divisions, with the officers, and the Ensign with the Standard in the centre. Eight Yeomen Warders from the Tower of London 'hold the base', the one occasion on which they parade with the Yeomen of the Guard.

As the Queen appears, she is greeted with a Royal salute, and carries out the inspection. The Yeomen then give 'Three Cheers for Her Majesty', before marching proudly past to the strains of *The British Grenadiers*.

It is very much a personal affair, as the Monarch reviews her own loyal and long-established Body Guard, watched only by friends and relatives of the Yeomen, and it is perhaps the most valued of the special Body Guard occasions.

The Roger Monk Dinner

Roger Monk was a successful nineteenth century businessman in London, who was in 1826 Master of the Tallow Chandlers' Company. He purchased a commission first with the Gentlemen at Arms, and then in the Body Guard where he became Exon in 1805, an appointment he held until his death in 1831. He was extremely proud of his position as Exon, and had a portrait painted of himself in the magnificent Tudor-style uniform that was worn by the officers of the Guard for the Coronation of George IV in 1821.

The Roger Monk Dinner, 1958.

Tudor uniform from the reign of Edward VI. The uniform worn by Roger Monk and the other officers of the Guard at the Coronation of George IV in 1821 was an extremely ornate version of the clothing worn by Yeomen at this time.

He must have been wealthy, for that uniform cost the then very large sum of £300; but he was also very generous and made several bequests to charities. Among others he left two annuities of £20 a year, one to the Gentlemen at Arms and one to the Yeomen of the Guard, as recorded in their Order Book under 19 September 1837:

Roger Monk, Esquire, formerly an Exon of the Yeomen of the Guard, and who died in the month of October 1831, by his will dated 10 April 1828, gave the residue of his estate and effects to the Tallow Chandlers' Company of the City of London, subject to the payment by them and their successors of [amongst other things] an annuity of £20 per annum, to be paid to the two senior Ushers of the Body Guard of the Yeomen of the Guard for ever, towards the expense of a dinner annually in honour of His Majesty's birthday.

This bequest continues today and is much appreciated, although the annuity now goes little further than paying for the port at the dinner, which is held every year. It is very properly called the Roger Monk Dinner, and is attended by all members of the Body Guard, past and present; after the Loyal Toast has been drunk, glasses are raised to the memory of Exon Roger Monk.[17] The Gentlemen at Arms also drink a toast to Roger Monk at their dinner, in appreciation of his bequest to them.

Anniversaries

During their existence the Yeomen of the Guard have been able to celebrate no fewer than four centenaries, and are on the verge of their fifth, which promises to be the best yet. It is intriguing to look back and see what life was like as far as the Yeomen were concerned on each of the four centenaries to date.

1585. This was the twenty-seventh year of the reign of that great Tudor Queen, Elizabeth I, and it was a troubled time. Relations were strained between England and Spain, her traditional foe, and the drama and danger of the Spanish Armada was only three years away. Ireland was an increasing worry, and a detachment of 60 Yeomen was stationed there with the Viceroy, Sir Henry Sidney. There were also 30 Yeomen guarding Mary, Queen of Scots at Tutbury Castle 'as a perpetual watch and ward'.

There were threats against the life of Elizabeth, and she therefore had a very real need of the protection provided by her Yeomen,

---

[17] Roger Monk is buried in the cloisters of Westminster Abbey, where a marble tablet on the wall and a gravestone in the pathway mark his resting place.

who were about 100 strong, half mounted and half on foot. They wore much the same uniform as today but with a different head-dress, and they had Royal initials on their doublets for the first time, as well as the ruffs that the Queen had introduced.

The Captain of the Guard was the celebrated Sir Christopher Hatton, the seventeenth Captain, who had taken over in 1572, and would, the next year, be promoted to Lord Chamberlain and so leave the Body Guard.

It is not surprising that, in view of the troubles facing the country, there was no special centenary celebration that year, though doubtless the Yeomen received an extra ration of beef and ale!

1685. By now the House of Tudor had been succeeded by the Stuarts, and James II had just come to the throne. The first part of the year was dominated by his Coronation on 23 April, and the Yeomen of the Guard were present in their traditional role.

The Captain of the Guard (the twenty-fifth) was George Villiers, 4th Viscount Grandison, who had taken over in 1662 under Charles II, and would continue into the reign of William and Mary, until 1689.

Again, there do not seem to have been any special celebrations for their bicentenary.

1785. By the time the Body Guard reached their tercentenary the Stuarts had given way to the House of Hanover; George III (1760–1820) was on the throne and was entitled to celebrate his own Silver Jubilee. But there were, in fact, few festivities, for it had not yet become fashionable to celebrate Royal Jubilees.

The Captain of the Guard (the forty-first) was Heneage Finch, Earl of Aylesford, who had been appointed the previous year, and would continue in the post for 20 years, until appointed Lord Steward in 1804.

He was, as are his family today, enthusiastic about archery, and so it is not surprising that the Yeomen celebrated their tercentenary with an archery contest which consisted of a match with the long-bow between ten chosen Yeomen. It was at 'point blank 100 yards' and the Captain awarded prizes for the three top scores. The first was a silver cup of a value of twenty guineas, the second was ten guineas in money and the third prize was three guineas. The cup was suitably inscribed and was won by Yeoman Ralph Cothard, but has unfortunately since disappeared.

1885. The Body Guard have been remarkably unlucky with the timing of their anniversaries, for their 400th in 1885 saw a change in the Captaincy, which threatened even the annual Inspection, let alone any quatercentenary celebrations.

William Payn, a Yeoman of the Guard, 1568. From a rubbing from his tomb brass at West Wickham, Kent.

The sixty-first Captain, since 1880, had been Lord Monson (afterwards Viscount Oxenbridge) but in June 1885 there was a change of Government and, being one of the Deputy Chief Whips, Monson had to resign as Captain of the Guard on 29 June. He was replaced by Viscount Barrington who, in fact, held the post for only eight months before he too had to resign and Lord Monson returned (as the sixty-third Captain) having missed half the centenary year.

Due perhaps to these upheavals, there were no particular celebrations for this anniversary, but one all-important event followed soon after, which was the writing of *The History of the King's Body Guard of the Yeomen of the Guard* by Colonel Sir Reginald Hennell, who was Clerk of the Cheque from 1895.

1985. It would be foolish to try to forecast events in 1985 when the Yeomen celebrate their 500th anniversary, but it does look from the planning as if the event will be bigger and better than any of the four previous occasions – which is entirely as it should be.

Looking ahead, the Captain is likely to be the ninety-second or ninety-third. A new Standard is due to be presented by the Sovereign at her Inspection of the Body Guard that year. The Yeomen should be up to strength and in very good heart, and they will doubtless find ways of marking this historic year in an appropriate manner.

Looking back, what are the landmarks of the last hundred years for the Yeomen? There have been two World Wars, in both of which the Yeomen have played a worthy part. The great British Empire of Queen Victoria has become the Commonwealth of another Queen. Since 1938, the Ensign has had a Standard to carry (for the first time in 130 years). The Yeomen now wear nylon and gold thread on their doublets instead of pure gold braid, and their ranks include fighting men unknown to the Victorians, such as tank drivers, parachutists, pilots and radio operators.

Above all, the way of life has changed more than in any other one hundred years. In 1885 the Yeomen had to read by gaslight, travelled in horse-drawn buses or at best by train and there were virtually no telephones. The wars they fought were little different from those of 1785 or even 1685. They knew nothing of aeroplanes or anaesthetics, submarines or satellites, cars or computers. It was a remarkably different world.

Yet certain things have not changed since 1885 – or indeed since 1585 – the character of the Yeomen themselves; their loyalty to the Crown, their spirit of duty and discipline; and their pride in being members of the Queen's Body Guard.

8

Uniform

It would be pleasant to be able to say that the splendid uniforms worn today by the Yeomen of the Guard and their officers are the same as those designed for them by their founder, King Henry VII. But as we have seen, they then wore only simple russet cloth, and it was his son, Henry VIII, who in his customary flamboyant style provided them, in about 1510, with the 'rich coats' for which they are so well known now. Even then, the ruffs and the round, velvet bonnets did not appear until later, and there have been many changes over the years in the uniform of both the officers and the Yeomen.

Officers' Uniforms

In Tudor times, the officers of the Guard probably wore a uniform along the same lines as that of the Yeomen today, though there are sadly no records to confirm this. Then in the seventeenth and eighteenth centuries, a wide variety of uniforms developed, based mainly on the whims of the individuals and the fashions of the time.

Things became particularly out of hand during the late eighteenth century when the Body Guard lost its military background, and consisted of civilians who dressed themselves in decidedly exotic outfits. William IV put an end to this by declaring that, as the officers of this Guard were in future to be former Regular Army officers, they should therefore wear some form of military uniform, and he chose that of a field officer in the Foot Guards, but with a cocked hat rather than a bearskin and with the addition on the collar and cuffs of the rose, thistle and shamrock.

This is still the officers' uniform today, and each one would now cost over £3,000. Each set is therefore carefully treasured, and handed on from officer to officer, with whatever alterations are essential. Some official help is granted to officers needing to purchase a new uniform and it is gratefully received.

A sword is part of the uniform, but is never drawn except when the Body Guard are on parade for their Annual Inspection. There are legends about occasions on which swords could not be extracted from their scabbards at the crucial moment, and one officer is even said, long ago, to have drawn only a somewhat rusted six inch stump of a blade!

Earl Waldegrave, Captain of the Guard 1896–1906, in uniform, with his wand of office.

The officers also carry an ebony wand of office, which is presented to them personally by the Sovereign on appointment; should they leave or be promoted, they hand back their wand of office and, if appropriate, receive a new one. The Captain once had a richly chased gold head to his wand, but today it is silver for all the officers.

At the Coronation of King George IV in 1821, the officers of the Guard appeared in a new and most impressive Tudor style uniform, very similar to that worn by the Yeomen today. It is not known whether this uniform was ever worn in Tudor times or whether it was simply the imaginative creation of the Norman Hartnell of 1821. Whatever the answer, this one ceremony seems to have been the first and the last time that this splendid order of dress was seen, for William IV said firmly in 1831 '... the state coronation dress of the officers of the Yeomen of the Guard shall be discontinued until further orders.' It has not been worn since, though there was some discussion in 1902 as to whether it might be revived. It was eventually decided that, 'though from a historical point of view the change might seem to be appropriate, the fact of the present uni-

Four officers and a sergeant of the Body Guard, c 1900, showing the various uniforms, described by Colonel Hennell in his history as 'a modern group'!

Three distinguished post-war officers of the Body Guard Left: Lieutenant-Colonel VB Turner, VC, Clerk of the Cheque. Centre: *Major-General Sir Allan Adair, CB, CVO, DSO, MC, Lieutenant.* Right: *Lieutenant-Colonel J Hornung, OBE, MC, Exon.*

form having been adopted especially when the officers began to be appointed from the Regular Army, outweighed it.'

Yeomens' Uniforms

As mentioned in Chapter 2, the Yeomen did not get their scarlet doublets until Henry VIII's reign, and before that they wore russet cloth for everyday work, and a uniform of Tudor white and green for ceremonial occasions.

During the reign of Henry VIII, the Yeomen had three distinct uniforms, headed by a magnificent 'rich coat' of Royal scarlet and gold, much like that worn today. According to the Household Book of Henry VIII, it was 'guarded and faced with dark-blue velvet, and on their breasts and backs the union rose and over it the royal crown embroidered in gold'.

The second uniform in use at this time was the Tudor white and green livery which was probably used most of the time at Court (other than on special State occasions) and it continued to be worn until about 1530. In 1514, the Duke of Suffolk, when Ambassador to France, was allowed an escort of 18 Yeomen of the Guard, and they were clothed in 'white and green satten [their normal wear] … and like quantities of scarlet cloth [their state coats] …'

Finally, the Yeomen kept their doublets of russet cloth as their working dress. These were particularly needed when they travelled round the Kingdom with Henry VIII; while the King and others rode in carriages or on horseback, some Yeomen usually marched along in the dust or mud, for which they sensibly wore their russet cloth.

Their 'rich coats', together with the Standards of the Guard, were carried on carts. In 1510 one contractor was paid *2d* a mile for this job during a Royal progress from London to Dorset and back, a trip that he covered at some 12 miles a day. And in 1538 there are entries in the Household Books about 'rooms to house the great standards and women to brush and ayre [air] the rich coates of the Garde'.

Two items of 'special clothing' in use by the Yeomen at this time are worthy of mention. The first is some type of light armour, worn when they went campaigning in France.

The second item is a special doublet, issued to the Yeomen for wrestling. This was one of the skills expected of them, and the King enjoyed calling on them to compete for his entertainment. In 1532, for example, a Royal Warrant was made out, 'To Parker, Yeoman of the Robes, for doublettes for the Garde to wrestle before the French King at Calais 44*s* 8*d*.' When Henry VIII and Francis I met, a challenge was issued for a contest between their households, and it is recorded that, 'The French King had none but priests that wrestled, which were big men and strong, they were taller but they had most falls.' So presumably the Yeomen won, and justified the expense of their special doublets.

The headdress at this time seems to have been either a floppy black cap or a bonnet with a small brim; both were adorned on occasions with a feather, and in general the rules governing headdress of the period were fairly flexible.

There was no significant change in the uniform during the brief reigns of Edward VI and Mary, but several major innovations were made by Queen Elizabeth. First, she introduced the ruff (though this was replaced under the Stuarts by a linen collar; it was then reintroduced by Queen Anne and is still worn today).

Elizabeth also had the Sovereign's initials embroidered on the State livery from about 1570; it is possible that this may have been done earlier, but there is no record of it. Finally, she replaced the previous bonnet with a befeathered velvet hat.

Mounted Yeomen wore roughly the same dress as Yeomen on foot, and there is a good picture of one in State livery in a drawing

A Yeoman in the time of Queen Mary, showing how uniform followed the fashions. From a contemporary drawing.

*Yeomen on duty with partisans
and swords at the Royal Italian
Opera, Covent Garden,
during the reign of Queen
Victoria.*

published in 1575; though the uniform shown probably dates
from before 1570, as there are no Royal initials on it.

The Stuarts substantially changed the uniform of the Yeomen,
not only by abandoning the ruff, in favour of a lace collar, but also
by adopting the Cavalier-style broad-brimmed hats, at least for the
second livery. They also substituted St Edward's crown for the
Tudor crown, and since then the crown used in the Royal coat of

arms has changed at intervals, as decided by the Monarch in each reign.

James I added the Royal motto *Dieu et mon Droit* to the insignia. He might have been expected to add also the thistle of Scotland, being himself James VI of Scotland, but did not do so and that was left for Queen Anne to do, following the Union of 1707.

The main event of Charles II's reign, as far as dress was concerned, was that he introduced the present style of hat for the Yeomen. A draft Order in Council of 22 October 1680, described it as 'black fluted velvet, low crowned, flat brim, ornamented with a band of coloured ribbons, red, white and dark blue, tied up in bows and fastened on a plaited cord.'

According to a Royal Warrant of 10 October 1671, the waist belts at this time were buff, and they did not become the present gold and black until 1742.

The reign of William and Mary is of interest, because they both had their initials embroidered on the Yeomen's coats, the only time this has happened.

Queen Anne added the thistle to the emblem on the Yeomen's coats in 1707, and George III completed the emblem by including

The Yeomen of the Guard, 1900, when they all wore beards. It is said that Ismail Pasha, the viceroy of Egypt, was so impressed by the stern appearance of Queen Victoria's Yeomen that he provided his own bodyguard with false beards in an attempt to render them as impressive.

Members of the Body Guard, c 1959. All were former members of the Household Division.

the shamrock following the Union with Ireland in 1801. He also ordered the wearing of wigs, which accorded with the fashion of the time.

George IV, at his extravagant Coronation in 1821, clothed the officers of his Guard in the Tudor-style uniform already described, but made no changes to the dress of the Yeomen. He did, however, initiate a grant of £9 to every Yeoman in lieu of his old uniform which had until then become his personal property when it was replaced every year. This was apparently necessary 'to prevent the dresses being bought up by persons for theatrical or other public exhibitions.' This allowance was continued until c 1831, when the duties of the Yeomen became much lighter and the wear and tear on their uniforms correspondingly less; new uniforms were thenceforth issued only when required rather than automatically every year.

Since then there have been only minor changes in the uniform of the Yeomen. Happily they still wear the splendid Tudor 'rich coats' on which are embroidered the history of our country for the past 500 years—the crown, the rose of England, the thistle of Scotland, the shamrock for Ireland and the Tudor crown for Wales.

9

Organisation

Chapter 2 described the organisation of the Body Guard during the first 25 years of its life. We now bring the story up-to-date.

Organisation

1509–1669. The accession of King Henry VIII in 1509 meant several changes for the Yeomen of the Guard. For a start their numbers were increased, because the King was either fighting the French or trying to outdo them in the magnificence of his Court.

It was as part of this rivalry that Henry VIII created in 1509 his second Royal bodyguard, 'The Gentlemen Spears'. They were socially superior to the Yeomen, in that they were 'cadets of noble families and the higher order of gentry', and as such they were given precedence over the Yeomen of the Guard, who thus also lost their privileged position as the Nearest Guard.

Today 'The Honourable Corps of Gentlemen at Arms', as they have been called since 1834, are the senior Royal bodyguard, even though they were formed 24 years later than the Yeomen.

To the Yeomen, the loss of their position as the Nearest Guard was a bitter blow, and they accepted the situation reluctantly. Indeed, the matter was still being raised nearly 350 years later when, in 1851, all the precedents were examined in detail and a final ruling was given by Queen Victoria herself to the effect that:

'... *the Corps of Gentlemen at Arms whenever we shall command their attendance shall do the duty of the Guards nearest to our Royal person and shall attend for the purpose of performing such duty when so commanded upon all State occasions whether in our Royal Palaces or elsewhere and that the Yeomen of the Guard shall be the Corps upon all such occasions doing duty next to the Corps of Gentlemen at Arms.'*[18]

For the first 250 years of their existence the Yeomen of the Guard were, as we have seen, primarily a fighting organisation, with a Captain who was in effect their military commander. During the sixteenth century he was usually a knight, and this period

[18] Letter: Lord Chamberlain to the Captain of the Gentlemen at Arms, 11 July, 1851.

Sir Walter Raleigh, Captain of the Guard, at the Funeral of Queen Elizabeth I in 1603. The Yeomen wear the black 'caules' that are still worn today at Royal funerals. From a drawing in the Rothschild Collection, now in the British Museum.

saw several outstanding figures, headed by Sir Christopher Hatton, who was Captain from 1572 to 1579, and Sir Walter Raleigh, who was Captain on three separate occasions.

The life of Sir Christopher Hatton was a remarkable one. He emerged from obscurity when, as a law student in 1568, he attracted the attention of Queen Elizabeth by his talent and good looks while performing in a masque in the Temple. He was given a position in the Household and was then made a Gentleman Pensioner; his next post was Gentleman of the Privy Chamber, followed in 1572 by Captain of the Guard. A set of his armour, dated 1580, is in the Royal Collection at Windsor Castle. Knighted in 1581 he became Lord Chancellor six years later, which meant he must cease to be Captain. He became also a Privy Councillor, a Knight of the Garter, and a very powerful figure at Court.

He used his powers to acquire Ely Palace, which he fancied as his own residence. The Bishop objected, whereupon Sir Christopher sought the Queen's support, and she wrote the famous epistle, 'PROUD PRELATE—You know what you were before I made you what you are now: if you do not immediately comply with my request, by God! I will unfrock you. ELIZABETH.

When Sir Christopher died as a bachelor in 1591 he was given a State funeral and buried in St Paul's Cathedral.

Sir Walter Raleigh was a very different character. Born in 1552 at the farmhouse of Hayes near Budleigh Salterton in Devon, he was a dashing, gallant adventurer throughout his life. At the age of 17 he fought as a volunteer in France on the side of the Huguenots, and then in Ireland where his exploits brought him to the attention of the Queen in 1578. She installed him at Court, but it was not to his liking and he was restless; so in 1586 she made him Captain of the Guard in order to keep him near her.

In 1592, however, he incurred her Royal wrath by having an affair with one of her maids-of-honour, Elizabeth Throgmorton, and they were both promptly despatched to the Tower. Raleigh was released a few months later, but was not forgiven and was not reinstated as Captain. He spent the next five years keeping out of the way by embarking on expeditions to America and on forays against Spain; then in an attack on Cadiz in 1597, he earned such fame for his courage and leadership that he was restored to favour and reinstated as Captain of the Guard.

But his troubles were far from over. On the death of the Queen in 1603, he was accused of being involved in the plot to place Arabella Stuart on the throne in place of James VI of Scotland. He was found guilty, and was once again escorted to the Tower by his own Yeomen, having for the second time been deprived of his post as Captain.

This time he remained imprisoned for 13 long years, only being released in 1616 in order to lead a doomed expedition that James I wanted to send to Guiana in South America in search of gold. Although he was now aged 65, Raleigh set off, happy to be free at last but the venture was not successful and the King was angry and disappointed. When Raleigh returned, he was again sent to the Tower, for the third and last time.

He was executed on 19 October 1618, meeting his death with typical courage and bravado. He felt the blade of the axe to test its sharpness, and when the executioner hesitated, he exclaimed, 'What dost fear? Strike, man, strike.'

During the seventeenth century, the responsibilities of the Captain diminished, and the post became a prestige appointment, held by a peer and given to ministers and members of the Court. The Captain also ceased to be Vice-Chamberlain, and so had fewer duties at Court.

The officers of the Guard during this period were the Captain, the Clerk of the Cheque and the Standard Bearer. There was no Lieutenant and the post of Exon had not yet been created.

The number of Yeomen varied considerably. Under Henry VII they totalled up to 126, but Henry VIII promptly increased this to 200. When he went to war against France in 1513 the strength of the Guard was increased to 600, and they thus became an effective fighting unit. Once the campaign was over, peacetime economies had – as always – to be undertaken and under the *Statutes of Eltham* in 1526 some 400 Yeoman were pensioned off as Yeomen of the Crown, leaving the Guard 200 strong again. Under Queen Elizabeth the number was fixed at around 100, where it remained until 1669, except for variations during the Civil War of 1642–1649, and the exile of Charles II from 1649–1660, when it decreased substantially.

During the sixteenth and seventeenth centuries, the rank of Yeoman of the Guard was filled by men of much the same class as those in the time of Henry VII. The position was undoubtedly one of honour, and the practice of purchasing an appointment, either as an officer or a Yeoman, was already prevalent. James I did not approve and laid down in 1610, '... that these places of my Guard be not traffickt or sould, but freely disposed of for meritt and sufficiency, for otherwise it must needs be a hindrance to my service to have them impoverished by purchasing their places in a mercinary manner.'

1669–1813. In 1669, King Charles II reorganised the Body Guard along the military lines of the day, and according to the Council Register for 29 October 1669 the new establishment was:

That there be one Captain of the said Guard at the yearly pay of £1,000.
A Lieutenant at £500 per ann.
An Ensign at £300 per ann.
A Clerk of the Cheque at £150.
Four Corporals, each at £150 per ann.
One Hundred Yeomen in daily waiting, each at £30 per ann.
Seventy Yeomen not in waiting, each at £15 per ann. Which said several sums amount in the whole unto £6,600 yearly.
And when any of the said number of one hundred die, that their

Lieutenant, Ensign and Body Guard at the time of the Coronation of King James II, 1685.

places be filled up out of the seventy not in waiting, and that if any of the seventy die that no more be admitted in their rooms. The King directed the Captain to remodel the Band accordingly.

The organisation of the Guard has changed remarkably little during the last 300 years, and it is interesting to compare the present establishment with that of 1669 and even with what it may have been in 1486.

Appointment	1486	1669	1984
Captain	1	1	1
Lieutenant		1	1
Clerk of the Cheque	1	1	1
Standard Bearer/Ensign	1	1	1
Junior Officers	?	4 (Corporals)	2 (Exons)
	3 (?)	8	6
Ushers	?	8	-
Messenger Sergeant Majors	?		2
Divisional Sergeant Majors	?		4
Yeomen	120[1]	92	60
Exempt List			15
	120	100	81

[1] This probably included some NCOs.

In 1669 the Clerk of the Cheque was junior to the newly-created Ensign, the former Standard Bearer. This was changed, however, in 1927, and he now ranks immediately after the Lieutenant.

The new and rather unusual rank of 'Corporal', created in 1669, was the forerunner of the rank of Exon, and it has an involved history.

When Charles II reorganised the Guard, and also his Army, he took as his model the French Army, which he had come to know all too well during his exile in France, just as Henry VII had done 170 years before. The appointment of *Corporal* in France was a commissioned rank roughly equal to captain (which is how Napoleon Bonaparte later came to be known as *le petit caporal*). It was logical therefore for Charles II to introduce that rank when he wanted some junior officers in the Body Guard; he also used it when he created The Life Guards in 1661.

Another term in use in the French Army at this time was *Exempt* or *Exoneré*, which was applied to officers who were doing duty away from their regiment. Some of the corporals of the Body Guard may well have come into this category, and thus they came

18 The Yeomen of the Guard in their traditional place, at the rear of the Garter procession, immediately behind the Sovereign. Once the procession has arrived at St George's Chapel for the Garter Service the Yeomen remain on guard inside the door until the service is ended.

19 The Queen alongside Colonel Brassey, Lieutenant of the Yeomen of the Guard, on the terrace steps of Buckingham Palace, 3 June 1982.

20 The Queen inspects her Body Guard, accompanied by Colonel Brassey, 3 June 1982.

21 *Opposite:* The development of the embroidered symbols on the coats of the Body Guard, 1603 – 1901.
1) Stuart period – St Edward's crown, rose, and initials.
2) William and Mary – the only instance of the King and Queen's initials being embroidered together.
3) Anne – reverts to Tudor crown, and adds thistle, 1709.
4) George III – St Edwards's crown, shamrock added, 1801.
5) Victoria.
6) Edward VII – reverts to Tudor crown, 1901.

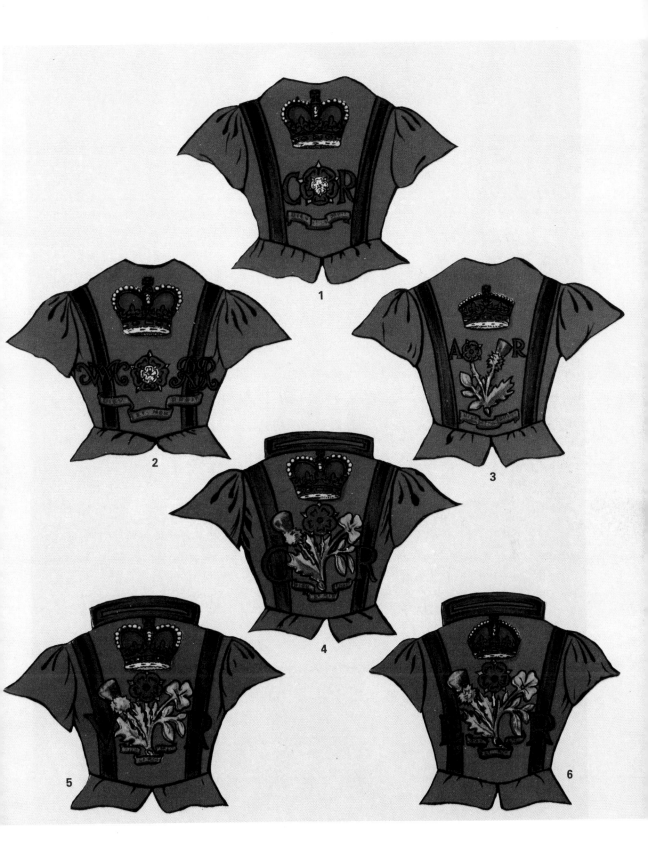

23 A Yeoman with partisan and sword, 1806. A watercolour from Colonel Sir Reginald Hennell's *History of the Guard*.

24 Sir Thomas Seymour Sadler, Exon of the Guard. In the new uniform for officers of the Body Guard, ordered by William IV, 1830-31.

22 *Opposite:* Roger Monk founder of the dinner named after him. He became Exon of the Body Guard in 1805 and held the appointment until his death in 1831. He wears the Tudor-style uniform worn by officers of the Guard for the Coronation of King George IV. Painting by Henry Pickersgill, hanging in Tallow Chandlers Hall, London.

25 Yeomen of the Guard together with two Gentlemen at Arms.

26 Two Yeomen of the Guard, ex members of the RAF, standing in front of a Hawker Siddeley Argosy of the Queen's Flight. Members of the Air Force became eligible after World War Two and the first one was appointed in 1955.

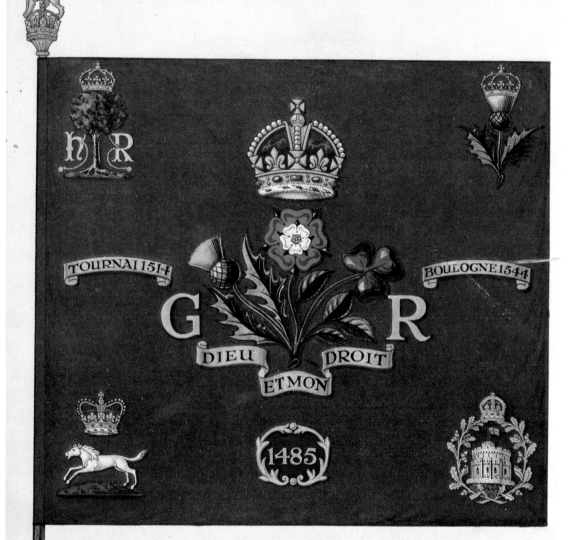

27 *Above:* The Painting of the Standard of the Body Guard approved by King George VI on 27 June 1938. It was based on a design drawn up by Garter, King of Arms.

28 Detail of the Standard, showing the badge of the House of Windsor, which did not exist until it was created so that it could represent the House of Windsor on the Standard of the Body Guard.

The State Opening of Parliament. Queen Victoria arrives at the Houses of Parliament accompanied by her Yeomen, 1880.

to be called *Exon*. Indeed, we find that they were for a time referred to by both titles, as for example in a warrant of 7 May 1711 which mentions, 'Horace Walpole Esq. appointed Corporal and Exon vice Davenant.'

Being the junior officers of the Guard, the Exons tended to bear the brunt of the duties (a position that they would probably say has not changed today !). Among their tasks was 'The Service of All Night' (see page 35); while the junior Exon has always been considered 'the most proper person' to conduct the Search.

During the eighteenth century the organisation of the Guard changed remarkably little, and even the Captains remained unaltered for long periods, to judge by a trio who managed between them to span no fewer than 83 years. They were:

Viscount Falmouth 1747–1782
The Earl of Aylesford 1783–1804
The Earl of Macclesfield 1804–1830

1813–1984. This period begins with the major change to the way of life of the Body Guard brought about by the decision that they should no longer live at Court.

When George, Prince of Wales, became Regent in 1811, the King's portion of the Guard was moved to Carlton House to attend the new Regent. For some time before that, a series of economies had been carried out in the Royal Household, and the number of people feeding at Court had been reduced to the point where the 30 Yeomen of the Guard on duty were now virtually the only staff still having their meals there. The had been eating at St James's Palace (and were not stinted) but now that they were at Carlton House, this was considered a suitable moment to end their meals at Court altogether. Board wages were given in lieu, and the 30 Yeomen on duty had to find their own rations instead of their traditional ration of 24 lb of beef a day.

Once they also ceased to live at Court, they were divided into four *Waits* or *Divisions*, who could each do the duties required in turn for a month at a time, and this system continues today.

The Exons also used to do duty for a month at a time, and lived in quarters in the Clock Tower of St James's Palace. An Exon in 1851 recorded that:

> *'The rooms in St James's Palace consist of a large sitting room, two bedrooms, antechamber and every convenience. They are on the first floor looking out upon St James' Street on one side and the Colour Court on the other ... They are furnished by the Crown and as much coal and candle as can be consumed is allowed.*
>
> *'The Exon on duty is responsible for the Guard [the Division of the Body Guard doing duty at that time, consisting of one Usher and 30 Yeomen] and should see the roll called at 12 noon every day, at the orderly room or Guard Chamber. During the drill season he should superintend the drilling of the men in the manual and platoon exercise and Company movements, which takes place twice a week for an hour each time in the Palace Garden ... The Exon commands the Guard on duty at Levées, Drawing Rooms, Receptions of Addresses, Ambassadors and other Foreigners of distinction, Court Balls, Concerts, Opening and Proroguing of Parliament, distribution of Queen's bounty at the Royal Chapels, or other places in State etc, etc, and his name is always mentioned in the Court Circular as having so commanded.*
>
> *There is a seat belonging to the Exon in the Chapel Royal.*
>
> *On State occasions, such as the Opening and Proroguing of Parliament etc, etc, the Exon has a seat in one of the Royal carriages with the other great officers of the Household and at other times is furnished with a horse from the Queen's Mews.'*

Exons are traditionally nominated by the Captain of the Guard, who puts forward several names to the Sovereign for each vacancy; he has the privilege of indicating which candidate is his personal preference, but the final choice rests, naturally, with the Monarch.

From the middle of the nineteenth century the appointment of

The Queen meets the officers of the Guard at her Inspection, 1962.

Captain of the Guard became increasingly political, and he began to be a peer nominated by the Government in power rather than by the Sovereign.

Two other major changes that occurred during that century were the ending of automatic knighthoods for officers of the Guard, and the abolition of the purchase of commissions. It had been traditional for one officer to be knighted on the occasion of a Coronation, and all the officers except the junior Exon could expect to receive a knighthood in due course, but this was ended by Queen Victoria in 1861.

Another custom that had existed since Stuart times was the purchase of appointments for agreed prices, a practice that occurred in the Services and other professions as well as in the Royal bodyguards. James I and Queen Anne are both on record as having protested against it, but apparently without being able to prevent it. William IV took a firm line, but it still took 25 years before it was phased out completely.

The prices paid for positions were substantial, and they were agreed officially under King William IV for compensation purposes. The Lieutenancy was valued at £8,000, the Exonship at £3,500, while the rank of Yeoman was worth £350.

In the case of the Yeomen, they themselves saw little of the £350; 300 guineas went to the Captain, because the gift of the appointment lay in his hands, ten guineas to the Clerk of the Cheque and one to his Deputy; five guineas were needed for the Captain's secretary and sixteen shillings for his servant; the clerks received five guineas and the messengers two.

The newcomer was also expected to give a 'treat' to the Guard which cost him five guineas, as well as paying ten shillings to the widow of his predecessor if the man had died in office. His pay was £45 per annum, so his initiation was fairly costly.

With the ending of purchase in 1861, the officers and the Yeomen of the Guard were once more selected – as specified by King James I – 'for meritt and sufficiency', and no longer 'in a mercinary manner'. And so it is still.

10

The Standard

From their creation, the Body Guard had a Standard that was carried both in battle and also on parade in peacetime, though the design on it is uncertain.

Then, in about 1805, the Captain, the Earl of Macclesfield, ordered '... that the Standard and the Books belonging to the Corps and kept by him should now be given up and be considered in future the property of the Corps and kept as such by the Secretary for the time being', at St James's Palace.

The timing of this change was most unfortunate, for only four years later, in January 1809, much of the Palace was burnt down in a disastrous fire which destroyed not only all the records of the Body Guard, but also its Standard.

The records were lovingly and laboriously re-constructed over a period of nine years (1895–1904) by Colonel Sir Reginald Hennell, who was Clerk of the Cheque at that time, and later wrote his definitive history of the Body Guard based on this research.

For some strange reason the Standard was not replaced for 130 years. Then, on 5 July 1938, King George VI presented a new Standard at a parade in the grounds of Buckingham Palace, and said in his speech, ' It is with sincere pride as well as pleasure that I inspect you and restore to you your Standard. For many years it has been missing from your ranks, but a century is only a fraction of the term of your loyalty and service to my ancestors ...'

The designing of the new Standard in 1938 had to be started virtually from scratch, and it is of particular significance in that it can fairly be said to have led to the creation of the badge of the House of Windsor.

A design was prepared in the normal manner by Garter, King of Arms, and submitted to the King for approval. It showed the badges of Henry VII, James I, the House of Hanover and the initials 'V.R.' for Queen Victoria in the corners. The reply received was that the King wished two changes to be made.

'... the cypher 'V.R.' in the bottom right-hand corner is incorrect,' read the letter, 'since Queen Victoria was a member of the House of Hanover. The House of Windsor, His Majesty feels, should be represented in this corner of the Standard. Unfortunately there is no existing badge for the House of Windsor, and The King wishes Garter to design one representing the Round Tower

Above: The Ensign with the Standard and his Escort of two Yeomen.

The Ensign, the Standard of the Body Guard, in Colour Court at St James's Palace, 1960.

with the Royal Standard flying at the mast-head and the crown on top of it.'

Garter duly did as required, adding to the design a choice between antlers and oak leaves, as being appropriate for the House of Windsor, and was told, 'The King approves the design with the oak leaves round it for the Badge of the House of Windsor.'

'There is, however, one alteration,' the letter continued, 'which His Majesty would like to be made, and that is for the Flag to be depicted flowing, instead of the rather tinny and rigid object that it looks at present. As a sailor also, His Majesty would like it to be properly hoisted, that is right up to the top of the Flagpole.'[19]

This seems to have upset Garter somewhat, and he replied to the Lord Chamberlain, 'Perhaps you would explain to The King that I am anxious to show the whole of the Standard with as little crumpling of it as possible, both because any great movement in it distorts its component Coats, and also because, if fully shewn, it counteracts the effect of the small turret and mast being on one side. You will see that the centre line of the whole design runs through the middle of the flag.'

'As now altered, I think the flag is as it would appear at the moment when it is blown out to the full extent in a wind just strong enough to blow it out'. He then added somewhat plaintively, 'I spent some time yesterday studying flags in such a wind.'[20]

His pleas were accepted, and his design was finally approved on 27 June 1938. A painting was made of the design and submitted to the Privy Council, who duly gave it their approval. Thus, at a stroke, the Body Guard had a new Standard and the House of Windsor had its Badge.

[19] 25 May, 1938. Letter from the Lord Chamberlain to Garter, King of Arms.
[20] 23 June, 1938. Letter from Garter, King of Arms to the Lord Chamberlain.

11

The Yeomen of the Guard Today

The Body Guard has changed remarkably little in the last 150 years. As mentioned, the uniform is virtually the same as was introduced by King William IV in 1830 for both officers and Yeomen; the duties are purely ceremonial, as they have been since 1813; while the organisation is hardly changed from that laid down by Charles II over 300 years ago. Above all, the members of the Guard are men of the same calibre and character as those who were selected by William IV in the 1830s: then they were veterans of the Peninsular Campaign and Waterloo, and today they are veterans of World War Two and the campaigns round the world that followed.

The Officers

The Queen flanked by the Officers and Yeomen of Her Body Guard of the Yeomen of the Guard, 11 July 1974.

There are six officers in the Guard today, and their ranks are the same as in 1669, except that the number of Exons has been reduced from four to two, and the title of Adjutant has been added to that of the Clerk of the Cheque.

The Captain is still a 'political' appointment, and is traditionally

held by one of the Deputy Chief Whips of the House of Lords. (The Chief Whip is traditionally Captain of the Gentlemen at Arms.) For five centuries the Captainship has been a man's post, but it is quite possible that in the future the Captain could be a peeress, as has already been the case with the Gentlemen at Arms.[21]

Once vital amid the darkness, the lamps are now carried by tradition and not necessity on the Search.

The other five officers are all retired Army officers, selected from a list kept by the Ministry of Defence. They are all part-time as far as their Body Guard duties are concerned, and their civilian occupations range from farming to the wine business.

The requirements for acceptance are that they should be under 55 on joining and must be over 5ft 10in tall, since it was decided in 1908 that this should be the minimum height, '... in order to match the Yeomen [since] the appearance of undersized officers would be marked and unsightly.'

The present Lieutenant is, as it happens, 6ft 5in, and he had a

---

[21] Baroness Llewelyn-Davies of Hastoe was Government Chief Whip in the House of Lords and Captain of the Gentlemen at Arms 1974–1979.

The Queen speaks at the
Guildhall luncheon in honour
of her Silver Jubilee, 1977.
Her Yeomens stand behind
her.

different problem on joining. The Messenger Sergeant-Major at
that time was 'Snowy' Baker, formerly Regimental Sergeant-Major
of the Welsh Guards, a great personality and a much respected
man. The new officer went to pay his respects to him, and was
promptly invited to stand on a height measure that was kept in the
office. He did so, and the result was greeted with evident satisfaction by 'Snowy' Baker.

'Six foot, five inches, Sir. That's all right, Sir. I'm six foot six
inches, and we can't have anyone in the Body Guard who's taller
than me, can we, Sir?'

The Yeomen

The active strength of the Body Guard is 66, made up of two
Messenger Sergeant-Majors, four Sergeant-Majors and 60 Yeomen.

The senior Messenger Sergeant-Major is the only whole-time
member of the Guard, and he is in overall day-to-day control. He is
responsible for the administration, correspondence and the keeping of all the rosters and records. He also acts as Wardrobe Keeper,
which means looking after all the uniforms and ensuring that they
are ready for use when Yeomen arrive from all over the country
and go straight on duty. To enable him to do this, he lives in an

apartment in St James's Palace, where all the belongings of the Guard are kept.

For the last 14 years this post has been held by RSM Cyril Phillips, MBE, formerly in the Welsh Guards. He crowned his 37 years of military service by holding the senior Warrant Officer's appointment in the British Army, that of Academy Sergeant-Major at Sandhurst from 1962 to 1971, when he joined the Body Guard. The second Messenger Sergeant-Major is his deputy, ready to take over at any time if necessary.

The four Sergeant-Majors are each in charge of one Division, and to assist them they each have a Yeoman Bed-Goer and a Yeoman Bed-Hanger. It is more than two centuries now since it was their duty to bounce on the Royal mattress or search the Royal bedroom for intruders, and these historic titles are held today by Yeomen who have earned them by long service in the Guard.

All ranks of the Guard retire at 70, by which time they will probably have completed some 50 years of service to the Crown; Yeomen then join the Exempt List, which means that for the rest of their days they are exempt from further duties, but remain on half-pay.

At the other end of the scale are the newcomers who replace them. They will be in their 50s when they join, and recently retired from the Armed Forces. Vacancies average three or four a year, and they are much sought after.

There are certain qualifications to be met, which are that any candidate must have been a sergeant or above in the Royal Marines, the Army or the Royal Air Force. He must be not less than 5ft 10in in height, and must have earned a Long Service and Good Conduct Medal. He was at one time also required to have at least one campaign medal, but this was dropped in the 1970s as being no longer feasible; preference is, however, given to those who have a good active service record.

There is no specified breakdown between the Services, and in 1983, for example, there were seven from the Royal Marines, three from the RAF and the remainder from the Army. Nor were all the Army members drawn from the Infantry. There were six cavalrymen, two gunners, three from the Royal Electrical and Mechanical Engineers and one from the Royal Army Ordnance Corps. There are several Yeomen who are entitled to wear a parachutist's badge, a sight that would surely have intrigued and delighted both their founder and his son, King Henry VIII. The final requirement for a Yeoman is that he must be smart and soldier-like on parade and able to drill.

Provided that a candidate meets these requirements, he can put his name down on the waiting list kept by the Ministry of Defence. In due course, if he is lucky, he will be told there is a vacancy. He is then required to pass another 'medical', after which he is summoned to St James's Palace for an interview with the Clerk of the Cheque.

The present holder of this ancient office is a former Colonel in the Coldstream Guards, with an MBE awarded for service in British Guiana, five medals from World War Two, as well as campaign medals for service in Palestine and Malaya. He is, in effect, the Adjutant—with all the paperwork that this involves—and he has to fit that in with his whole-time civilian job. He is, therefore, very dependent on the Messenger Sergeant-Major to keep him fully briefed and to cope with the day-to-day problems.

The Adjutant interviews all potential Yeomen, and if he considers them to be suitable, he forwards their details to the Lord Chamberlain, who then lays them before the Monarch. Every Yeoman is thus personally approved by the Queen before he joins her Body Guard.

In due course, if he is accepted, he reports again to the Clerk of the Cheque, this time to be sworn in. With his hand on a Bible, he swears an oath of loyalty that resounds with history and has a touch of the Tudors about it:

'I, —, sincerely promise and swear to serve Her Most Sacred Majesty ELIZABETH II, by the Grace of God of the United Kingdom and Northern Ireland, Queen, Defender of the Faith, Her Heirs and Successors lawful Kings and Queens of these Realms both faithfully and truly in the place and Office I am now called unto, and to be placed in, namely, as one of the Yeomen of the Guard of Her Majesty's Guard of Her Body in Ordinary, and in all things touching Her Honour and Safety, I shall neither myself do, or procure, or give consent to be done by any other, any manner of thing that shall, or may be prejudicial, or hurtful of Her Majesty's Person, Crown, or Dignity, or to any of the Royal Family. But if I shall hear of, or by any way understand any such, or that any manner of Bodily hurt, dishonour, or prejudice may be in agitation, contriving, or likely to happen, I shall do as much as in me lyeth to prevent, stop and hinder the same, and besides to disclose and discover it with all speed to Her Majesty, or to such of Her Majesty's Council as I can or may come next unto, or to some or one of my Officers on duty, and by all ways and means I can possibly, to cause the same to be made known.

The Loyal Toast at Guildhall in 1972, on the occasion of the Queen's Silver Wedding.

110

I swear to be obedient to my Captain and all other of my Officers, of the said Guard in all things concerning my office in Her Majesty's Service.

I shall keep the Queen's peace in my own person both in the Court, and all other places, as much as in me lyeth, and shall cause all others to do the same to the utmost of my power.

All these things I shall truly, faithfully and obediently keep and perform.

SO HELP ME GOD.'

As proof of his enrolment he receives a certificate declaring that he is now ' ... one of the Yeomen in Ordinary of Her Majesty's Body Guard of the Yeomen of the Guard...' (as opposed to the Yeomen Warders, who are 'Extraordinary'). Furthermore, the document states that he is ' ... to have, hold, exercise and enjoy the said Place, together with all Rights, Profits, Privileges and Advantages thereto belonging.'

There are no tangible 'profits' today, such as being able to sell his post. The only tangible 'right' is perhaps exemption from jury service. But the 'privileges' and 'advantages' are certainly there, arising from membership of the Royal Household and attendance at many great State occasions. It is still a position of honour and prestige, and only those who have shown themselves to be fully deserving of the appointment will be accepted.

Yeomen of the Guard are selected with care, and just one example from the Nominal Roll shows the high standards that are maintained. Yeoman Baker joined the Body Guard in 1963 after 26 years in the Army, where he had ended up as a Regimental Sergeant-Major in the Royal Tank Regiment. He had six World War Two medals including a Military Medal for gallantry; after the war he earned two campaign medals in Korea, a Long Service and Good Conduct Medal and a Jubilee Medal.

The Yeomen are naturally expected to maintain a high standard of drill and turnout, as the Messenger Sergeant-Major soon makes clear to every newcomer, whatever his former rank.

'First, we'll issue you with your uniform, and get it properly fitted. Then we'll have a couple of drill parades. You won't have had much practice with a partisan and a sword, I don't suppose. And it's not too easy either, with a doublet on and a ruff round your neck. You only get two sessions at it with me, one out of uniform and one in full dress. After that, you've got to be good enough to parade in front of the Queen.'

The issue of a uniform is quite a tricky business. The supply of new doublets is strictly controlled, and each one may have to last up to 50 years. Indeed there was a time after World War Two when

A rare event in these troubled times. An Investiture by the Queen in Northern Ireland in 1977.

the selection of Yeomen was governed partly by the need to find men who fitted the uniforms then in stock! New uniforms are made by the Savile Row tailors, Compton Sons and Webb, who do this 'By Appointment to The Queen'. The doublet in particular must fit perfectly, and their tailor soon ensures, with an experienced touch, that every fold and wrinkle disappears.

Until the early 1980s all the doublets were 'richly embroidered' by hand with gold braid, but this has now been abandoned in favour of nylon and gold thread, which costs much less and is far more easily produced.

Having been approved finally in his new uniform—and placed it safely in his own locker—the new Yeoman then has the first of his two drill parades, where he learns how to handle his partisan, adopting the old position of *Stand at Ease*, with his hands clasped in front of him, over the shaft of the partisan. Only when considered by the Messenger Sergeant-Major to be proficient in his arms drill and properly dressed in his doublet, will the new Yeoman be allowed to appear in public.

Whatever their civilian employment, the Yeomen of the Guard

*A West Indian version of the
Yeomen of the Guard
presented for the Queen on her
visit to Nassau in 1977. The
picture was sent, with Her
Majesty's compliments, to Her
Body Guard.*

must be available for duty with the Guard when required, and employers are always very understanding about this. The sort of men suitable for the Queen's service are also much in demand for posts requiring integrity and responsibility; some, for example, are on the staff of the Houses of Parliament, in the Law Courts, banks and Government departments; others are self-employed, running shops, pubs, or post offices; a few have done particularly well in new careers, and one is bursar of a college, while another is managing director of a large international steel firm.

There are some 30 occasions a year when Yeomen are on duty, but the entire Body Guard are seldom on parade together, except for inspections, and occasionally for a State visit. Special events such as a Coronation are different—and also rather rare (see Appendix E).

The normal programme follows a fairly strict pattern. The season starts with the *Epiphany Service* in January, and then six or seven Winter *Investitures*. Spring brings the *Maundy Service*, a *State Visit* and the annual *Muster or Inspection*. The *Garter Service* is in June, and in July there will be two *Investitures* and three

113

Garden Parties, where the Yeomen keep the ground for the Queen and members of the Royal Family. There is usually a second *State Visit* in the autumn, the *State Opening of Parliament*, five or six more *Investitures* and a *Diplomatic Reception* at Buckingham Palace.

The number of Yeomen required at each of these functions varies widely (see Appendix E), but on average each Yeoman will be called upon six to eight times a year. The rosters are kept by the Messenger Sergeant-Major, and about three weeks before each duty, he sends out a 'Duty Notice', warning the appropriate numbers to parade, including one Yeoman in Waiting (who reports just in case anyone fails to arrive on time for any reason).

Also enclosed with the summons will be a return railway warrant, a concession that dates back only to the 1970s; before when, the Yeomen had to pay their own fares to and from London; although one Yeoman lived in Scotland and another in the Channel Islands, this did not deter them. Allowances are now also paid to cover meals and overnight accommodation, where this proves necessary.

On arrival at St James's Palace, those for duty report in and then set about the business of getting dressed. This is an elaborate process taking up to 30 minutes and is virtually impossible without some help. The first items are the breeches and the red stockings, with red, white and blue rosettes fastened just below the knee. Next come the black, buckled shoes, known as Monk Shoes, after Exon Roger Monk. The ruff has to be tied from behind, but once that is done, the Yeoman can put on the heavy doublet of scarlet and gold, bearing back and front the magnificent Royal badge of the rose, thistle and shamrock, surmounted by a crown and flanked by the initials 'E.R.II'.

On his chest he wears his medals, and slung over the left shoulder is the red, black and gold cross-belt that once carried the arquebus. From his waist belt hangs a sword, though this is never drawn. The black velvet hat, bedecked with red, white and blue ribbons round the crown, is almost the last item to be donned.

Finally, having pulled on his white gloves, the Yeoman collects his partisan, with the Royal arms and 'E.R.II' engraved on the blade. Unlike the uniforms, the partisans do not belong to individual Yeomen, but are held in a pool, and some of them are well over 100 years old.

After a quick but thorough inspection by the Messenger Sergeant-Major, the Yeomen are ready for whatever the duty may be for the day. If it happens to be an Investiture, this means a detachment of one Sergeant-Major and four Yeomen. They are driven over to Buckingham Palace in one of the Royal carriages, usually a brougham, and at 1050 hours precisely they step off in slow time from the East Gallery and enter the Ball Room, where some 350 guests are seated. While the band play *Men of Harlech* in recognition of the Welsh origins of the Body Guard, they take up their positions on the dais, behind where the Queen will stand.

Soon after 1100 hours, the Queen enters and the Investiture begins. It is quite a strain for the Yeomen, as it involves standing motionless for up to an hour and a half .But it is an impressive occasion, for the 150 or so recipients of honours and awards represent a true cross-section of the people of the country—servicemen, sportsmen, politicians, businessmen, artists, heroes and heroines.

As one Yeoman commented, 'They're all people who have done their bit for their country, just as we have. It is nice to be there and see them.'

About 1230 the last individual has received his or her medal and shaken hands with the Queen. Everyone leaves, and the Yeomen march off, glad to stretch their stiff limbs. With one more duty completed, they return to the routine of civilian life.

Why do men want to become Yeomen of the Guard? It is not because of any financial incentive, for the pay is nominal. The reason why men are proud to belong to 'The Queen's Body Guard of the Yeomen of the Guard' is that they regard it as an honour and a satisfaction to continue to serve their Sovereign, as they have done already for many years in the Armed Forces. It is also an opportunity to continue to be with others who believe, as they do, in such qualities as loyalty, integrity and service to Queen and Country.

The proud title of Yeomen of the Guard has stood for these qualities for 500 years, and will doubtless continue to do so for many years yet.

Face to face with history. From a drawing by an officer of the Guard.

Appendix A

The Body Guard in 1485

Brown, William
Bagger, Robert
Burley, John
Byde, John

Carre, Henry
Carre, John
Cheseman, William

Edwardes, John

Frere, Richard
Fulbrook, Thomas
Frye, John

Gervoys, John
Gaywode, Thomas

Honry, John
Hoo, John

John, Stephen
Jay, Robert

Kyngman, Thomas

Lloid, Piers
Leche, Thomas
Ley, Henry

Maddockes, William

Owen-Ap-Griffith

Pigot, Richard
Palmer, Robert

Racke, William
Rese-Ap-Philip
Rigby, John
Rake, Richard
Rothercomme, John

Selman, Richard
Staypull, Richard

Thomas, John

Waghan, William
Walker, Robert
Wallshe, Robert
Wode, Thomas
Westbury, Thomas

Appendix B

Captains of the Guard since 1485

Lord de Ros, 54th Captain (1852) and 56th Captain (1858–9).

The Earl of Limerick, 65th Captain (1889) and 67th Captain (1895–6).

1	1485	Earl of Oxford
2	1486	Sir Charles Somerset
3	1509	Sir Thomas Darcy
4	1509	Sir Henry Marney
5	1512	Sir Henry Guilford
6	1513	Sir John Gage
7	1516[1]	Sir Henry Marney
8	1530[1]	Sir William Kingston
9	1539	Sir Anthony Wingfield
10	1550	Sir Thomas Darcy
11	1551	Sir John Gates (executed)
12	1553	Sir Henry Jerningham
13	1557	Sir Henry Bedingfeld
14	1558	Sir Edward Rogers
15	1558	Sir William St Loe
16	1566	Sir Francis Kno(l)lys
17	1572	Sir Christopher Hatton
18	1586	Sir Henry Goodyere
19	1586–1592	Sir Walter Raleigh
	1592–97	Imprisoned and deprived of appointment
	1597–1603	Reinstated (executed)
20	1603	Sir Thomas Erskine
21	1617	Sir Henry Rich
22	1632[1]	Lord Dupplin
23	1635[1]	Earl of Morton
24	1643	Earl of Norwich
25	1662	Viscount Grandison
26	1689	Earl of Manchester
27	1702	Marquess of Hartington
28	1707	Viscount Townshend
29	1711	Hon. Henry Paget, Lord Burton (1712) Baron Paget (1714), Earl of Uxbridge (1715)
30	1715	Earl of Derby
31	1723	Earl of Chesterfield
32	1725	Earl of Leicester
33	1731	Earl of Ashburnham
34	1737	Duke of Manchester
35	1739	Earl of Essex

36	1743	Lord Berkeley of Stratton
37	1746	Viscount Torrington
38	1747	Viscount Falmouth
39	1782	Duke of Dorset
40	1783	Earl of Cholmondeley
41	1783	Earl of Aylesford
42	1804	Lord Pelham
43	1804	Earl of Macclesfield
44	1830	Marquess of Clanricarde
45	1834	Earl of Gosford
46	1835	Earl of Courtown
47	1835	Earl of Gosford
48	1835	Earl of Ilchester
49	1841	Earl of Surrey
50	1841	Marquess of Lothian
51	1841	Earl of Beverley
52	1846	Viscount Falkland
53	1848	Marquess of Donegall
54	1852	Lord de Ros
55	1852	Viscount Sydney
56	1858	Lord de Ros
57	1859	Earl of Ducie
58	1866	Earl Cadogan
59	1868	Duke of St Albans
60	1874	Baron Skelmersdale
61	1880	Lord Monson
62	1885	Viscount Barrington
63	1886	Lord Monson
64	1886	Earl of Kintore
65	1889	Earl of Limerick
66	1892	Lord Kensington
67	1895	Earl of Limerick
68	1896	Earl Waldegrave
69	1906	Duke of Manchester
70	1907	Lord Allendale
71	1911	Earl of Craven
72	1915	Lord Suffield
73	1918	Lord Hylton
74	1924	Major-General Lord Lock
75	1925	Lord Desborough
76	1929	Lord Lock
77	1931	Captain Lord Strathcona
78	1934	Colonel Lord Templemore
79	1945	Lord Walkden
80	1949	Lord Shepherd
81	1949	Lord Lucas of Chulworth

82	1950	Lieutenant-Colonel The Earl of Lucan
83	1951	Lord Archibald
84	1951	Lieutenant-Colonel The Earl of Onslow
85	1960	Major The Lord Newton
86	1962	Colonel The Viscount Goschen
87	1964	Lord Bowles
88	1971	Colonel The Viscount Goschen
89	1972	Lord Denham
90	1974	Lord Strabolgi
91	1979[8]	Lord Sandys
92	1982	Earl of Swinton

[1] Date uncertain.

Appendix C

Chronology of Events in which the Yeomen of the Guard were involved 1485 to date

1483–1485 *Richard III*
           Henry Tudor in exile in France.
     1485 Battle of Bosworth Field. King's Body Guard of the Yeomen of the Guard formed.
1485–1509 *Henry VII*
     1487 Battle of Field of Stoke.
     1492 Siege and capture of Boulogne.
     1497 Battle of Blackheath.
1509–1547 *Henry VIII.*
     1509 Henry VIII creates the Royal Body Guard of Gentlemen Spears.
     1509 Twelve Yeomen of the Guard appointed as Yeomen of the Tower.
1513–1519 Capture and garrisoning of Tournai. TOURNAI 1514 (battle honour).
     1520 Field of the Cloth of Gold.
1544–1546 War against France. BOULOGNE 1544 (battle honour).
     1545 Sinking of the *Mary Rose*.
1547–1553 *Edward VI.*
     1550 Warders of the Tower allowed to wear the uniform of the Yeomen of the Guard.
1553–1558 *Mary I*
1558–1603 *Elizabeth I*
    c1570 Sovereign's initials added to Yeomen's doublet.
1603–1625 *James I*
           Dieu et mon Droit added to the doublet.
     1605 Gunpowder Plot.
1625–1649 *Charles I*
     1633 State Visit to Scotland.
1642–1649 Civil War
1649–1660 The Commonwealth. Charles II in exile, with the Body Guard.
     1660 The Restoration. Body Guard re-formed.
1660–1685 *Charles II*
     1669 New establishment for the Body Guard. Rank of Corporal or Exon created.
1685–1688 *James II*

1688–1702	*William and Mary*
1690	Battle of the Boyne.
1702–1714	*Anne*
1707	Thistle added to the doublet, on Union with Scotland.
1714–1727	*George I*
1727–1760	*George II*
1743	Battle of Dettingen.
	Continual escort on the Sovereign ended.
1760–1820	*George III*
1801	Shamrock added to doublet, on Union with Ireland.
1809	Records and the Standard burnt in fire at St James's Palace.
1811–1820	Regency
1813	Yeomen of the Guard cease to live at Court.
1820–1830	*George IV*
1823	State Visit to Scotland.
1830–1837	*William IV*
1830–1831	Body Guard to consist in future of former members of the Army or Royal Marines. New uniform for officers.
1837–1901	*Victoria*
1861	Purchase of commissions abolished.
1885	Inspection by the Queen at Buckingham Palace for the first time.
1901–1910	*Edward VII*
1904	History of the Body Guard written by Colonel Sir Reginald Hennell.
1910–1936	*George V*
1911	State Visit to Ireland. Investiture of The Prince of Wales.
1927	Clerk of the Cheque made senior to the Ensign.
1936	*Edward VIII*
1936–1952	*George VI*
1938	New Standard presented by King George VI.
1952	Accession of Queen *Elizabeth II*.

Appendix D
Roll of the Body Guard in 1984

CAPTAIN:
THE EARL OF SWINTON

LIEUTENANT:
Colonel HUGH BRASSEY, OBE, MC
Royal Scots Greys

CLERK OF THE CHEQUE AND ADJUTANT:
Colonel ALAN PEMBERTON, MBE
Coldstream Guards

ENSIGN:
Major BRUCE SHAND, MC
12th Royal Lancers

EXONS:
Captain SIR CHARLES McGRIGOR, BT
Rifle Brigade

Colonel GREVILLE TUFNELL
Grenadier Guards

MESSENGERS

RSM Cyril PHILLIPS, MBE .... Academy Sergeant-Major,
Welsh Guards

WARDROBE KEEPER
RSM Cyril PHILLIPS, MBE

FIRST DIVISION

Rank	Name		Former Rank and Regiment
Sergeant-Major	Charles CRICKMORE, RVM	RSM	Grenadier Guards
Yeoman Bed-Goer	Leslie TRIMMING	RSM	Coldstream Guards
Yeoman Bed-Hanger	William BRAMMER	SCM	Life Guards
Yeoman	Alexander HAMILTON	RSM	Scots Guards
,,	Harry WEBB	RSM	Welsh Guards
,,	Ernest WOODMAN, MBE	WOII	Blues and Royals
,,	Reginald WARBOYS	QMS	Royal Marines
,,	Dennis WILKINSON	RSM	Coldstream Guards
,,	Lawrence WILKINSON	RQMS	Coldstream Guards
,,	Alan WILLIAMS	CQMS	Welsh Guards
,,	John FREEMAN, BEM	WOI	Queen's Royal Irish Hussars
,,	Kenneth MOYLAN	WOI	Royal Artillery
,,	John WILLIAMS, BEM	CQMS	Welsh Guards
,,	Dennis TUBB	CSM	Welsh Guards
,,	Don CHARLES	RCM	Life Guards
,,	Jack WRAGG	CSM	Coldstream Guards

SECOND DIVISION

Rank	Name		Former Rank and Regiment
Sergeant-Major	Frederick LAING	RSM	Queen's Own Hussars
Yeoman Bed-Goer	John CAWTHORNE	SCM	Life Guards
Yeoman Bed-Hanger	Frederick BRUNTWELL	CSM	Welsh Guards
Yeomen	Donald DODSON	RCM	Life Guards
,,	Lionel ROSSITER, MBE	CSM	Coldstream Guards
,,	Charles HAZELL, BEM	QMS(S)	Royal Marines
,,	Ronald WALKERDINE	WOII	Royal Marines
,,	John WALMSLEY	RQMS	Grenadier Guards
,,	Alan CHEW	WO	1st Queen's Dragoon Guards
,,	John STANYARD	RSM	Grenadier Guards
,,	Wilfred HARDY, MBE	WO	Royal Air Force
,,	Neville TAYLOR	Staff/Cpl	Life Guards
,,	Eirwyn JONES	RSM	Welsh Guards
,,	Dennis VASEY	RSM	Scots Guards

THIRD DIVISION

Rank	Name	Former Rank and Regiment	
Sergeant-Major	Frank PICKFORD, RVM	RSM	Coldstream Guards
Yeoman Bed-Goer	Albert ADAMS, BEM	WOII	Norfolks
Yeoman Bed-Hanger	Edwin GRANT	RQMS	Grenadier Guards
Yeoman	Eric LLOYD	RCM	Life Guards
"	Murdo LEITCH, MBE	DSgt	Scots Guards
"	George KIRKHAM, MBE	RSM	Grenadier Guards
"	William DRAYNER	QMS	Royal Marines
"	John COOPER	WOII	Royal Horse Guards
"	Leonard CHARLESWORTH	CSM	Coldstream Guards
"	Walter BINT	(CDR) WOI	Royal Army Ordnance Corps
"	Herbert PENNINGTON, MBE	RSM	Welch Regiment
"	John TYACK	WO	Royal Guards
"	Leighton FICE	CQMS	Royal Welch Fusiliers
"	John CHRISTIAN	WO	Royal Air Force
"	Mike BARWELL	(CDR) WOI	Royal Army Ordnance Corps

FOURTH DIVISION

Rank	Name	Former Rank and Regiment	
Sergeant-Major	Kenneth EDGINTON	WOII	Royal Electrical Mechanical Engineers
Yeoman Bed-Goer	Frank LOBLEY	BSM	Royal Artillery
Yeoman Bed-Hanger	Frank HARDY, BEM	QMS	Royal Marines
Yeoman	George SARGEANT	CSM	Coldstream Guards
"	Drummond WINDOW, MBE	Sgt	Royal Air Force
"	John HOOK	WOI	Coldstream Guards
"	Tom TAYLOR, MVO, MBE	WOI	Grenadier Guards
"	Harold HOWARTH	WOII	Grenadier Guards
"	Richard GREEN	WOI	Royal Electrical Mechanical Engineers
"	Roy BARNETT	WOI	Royal Electrical Mechanical Engineers
"	David FROGGATT	WO	Royal Air Force
"	Alfred LAMING	CSgt	Royal Marines
"	Dermot KEATINGE, BEM	WOII	Royal Engineers
"	Dennis TOMLIN	WOI	17/21 Lancers
"	William DAVIS	RSM	Irish Guards

Appendix E
Body Guard Duties

Duty	Times a year	Attendance Officers	Attendance Sergeant-Majors	Attendance Yeomen
ANNUAL				
1 Epiphany Service	1		1	12
2 Investitures	13		1	4
3 Maundy Service	1	1	2	20
State Visit				
4 Arrival	2	3	2	26
5 Diplomatic Reception	2		1	8
6 State Banquet	2	1	2	24
7 Inspection	1	all	all	all
8 Garter Service	1	3	2	24
9 Garden Parties	3	all	2	16
State Opening of Parliament				
10 The Search	1	1	1	10
11 State Opening	1	4	2	24
12 Diplomatic Reception	1	1	1	16
OCCASIONAL				
13 Royal Opera House		1	2	20
14 Coronation		all	all	all
15 Royal Wedding		all	all	all
16 Royal Funeral		2	2	22
17 Investiture of the Prince of Wales		3	2	13

Acknowledgements

Many people have helped me to compile this history, and I am very grateful for their contribution. In particular, I am much indebted to Miss Anita Hewerdine, an expert on the Yeomen of the Guard under the Tudors, who is carrying out post-graduate research on this subject at the University of London; and who provided a great deal of invaluable material and information from original sources, as well as checking many references.

The Lord Chamberlain's Office have taken endless trouble in making their records available to me, whatever the pressures on them, and I am much indebted to Lieutenant-Colonel Sir John Johnston, and John Titman, Peter Hartley, Marcus Bishop and David Rankin-Hunt. Miss Jane Langton has also been most helpful, as always, over research into the Royal Archives.

Major-General Giles Mills, Resident Governor at the Tower of London, personally did much research and work for me on the Yeomen Warders, and Garter King of Arms has provided material about the Standard of the Body Guard.

The officers of the Body Guard have taken great trouble over answering endless questions and reading drafts, while Messenger Sergeant-Majors Phillips and Tyacke have both provided much useful information as well as many illustrations.

Finally, Mrs Penney has done the typing with great accuracy and speed.

PICTURE CREDITS

B/W photographs and illustrations are supplied by the following:

Reproduced by Gracious Permission of Her Majesty The Queen 27, 30, 53 (bottom), 54 (top), 55 (top & bottom), 64 (top & bottom), 66, 77 (bottom): Body Guard archives 17, 70 (top & bottom), 74, 79, 80 (top), 87, 91, 99, 102, 103, 110, 112: The British Library 93: Hennell 6, 8, 14, 15, 18, 35, 38, 40, 42, 46, 47, 49, 53, 57 (top & bottom), 59, 69 (top), 72, 73, 77 (top), 82, 85, 86, 88, 95, 117 (top & bottom): Keystone 75 (top & bottom), 78 (top & bottom) 106: Lawson 20, 36 (left & right), 45, 48, 80 (bottom): Mary Evans Picture Library 24, 25, 39, 60 (top & bottom), 61, 62 (top & bottom), 63, 89, 90, 97: Press Association 69 (bottom), 105, 107, 108, 113: Property Services Agency 13: Public Record Office 13, 19.

Crown copyright material in the Public Record Office is reproduced by permission of the Controller·of Her Majesty's Stationary Office.

Colour illustrations by kind permission of the following: plate numbers in **bold**

Reproduced by Gracious Permission of Her Majesty The Queen **2**, **3**, **7**, **12**, **13**: Body Guard archives **25**, **27**, **28**: Bridgeman Art Library **10**: Hennell **9**, **21**, **23**, **24**: Keystone Press Agency **1**, **17**: Mary Evans Picture Library **11**: Ministry of Defence **18**, **26**: The Press Association **14**, **15**, **16**, **19**, **20**: Property Services Agency **4**, **5**, **6**: Tallow Chandlers **22**: Mr Tyacke **7**.
Front Cover photograph by Mike Roberts.

Every effort was made to trace copyright to all material in this book. The publisher and author apologise if they have inadvertently failed to credit any ownership of copyright.

Index

Colour plates are given in **bold**

Adair, Sir Allan 7, 78, 87
Alexandra, of Denmark, Princess **11**
All Night, Service of 35, 97
Anne, Queen 88, 90, 99, 121
Anniversaries, Body Guard 67, 81–3
Apsley, Sir Allan 28
Archers, Royal Company of 58
Army, British 20, 28, 50, 76, 84, 91, 96, 106, 107–9, 121
Arundel, Earl of 41, 42
Aylesford, Earl of 82, 97, 118

Back Stairs Duty 42–3
Baker, Messenger Sergeant-Major 78, 107
Baker, Yeoman Charles 51, 111
Baker, Yeoman Thomas 51
Banquet, State 36, 61, 125
Barrington, Viscount 83, 118
Battle-Axe Guard 58–9
Battle Honours 45, 47, 120
Bed-Making, Royal 40–1
Beefeaters 9, 31–2, 59
Bellamy 73–6
Blackey, Yeoman B 51
Blackheath, Battle of 44, 120
Black Rod 75
Bosworth, Battle of 7, 10–15, 16, 44, 51, 120
Boulogne, Sieges of 44–5, 47, 120
Boyne, Battle of 50, 121
Brandon, Sir William 13
Brassey, Colonel Hugh **19, 20**
Bray, Sir Reginald 14
Broke, Thomas 19
Brown, Yeoman William 13, 15, 116
Buckingham Palace 23, 43, 52, 60–2, 78–9, 101, 114, 121, **17**

Captain of the Guard 16–18, 26, 28, 34, 45, 63, 76–9, 82–3, 85, 92–100, 105–7, 117–9, 122
Chamberlain, Lord 41, 71, 82, 92, 102–4, 109
Chamberlain, Lord Great 17, 73–4
Chamberlain, Vice 17–19, 94
Charles I, King 35, 38, 49, 58, 76, 120
Charles II, King 28, 30, 35, 50, 52, 53, 82, 90, 95, 96, 105, 120
Chartist Riots 37
Cheque, Clerk of the 19, 36, 63, 71, 83, 94–6, 100, 101, 105, 109, 122
Chief Yeoman Warder 25, 27, 30

Chivalry, Orders of 65–6
Civil War, English 49, 95, 120
Colman, George **9**
Copping, Yeoman John 41
Cornwallis, Earl 33
Coronations 14, 15, 17, 32, 52–4, 80, 82, 86, 95, 99, 113, 125, **11, 22**
Corporal 95–7, 120
Cothard, Yeoman 82
Court, Body Guard duties at 17–22, 27, 37, 38–43, 87, 92, 94
cease to live at 97–8, 121
Covent Garden 37, 89, 125
Crowns 14–15, 21, 89, **21**
Crown Jewels 30–31

Dartmouth, Lord 28
de Medici, Cosmo 31
de Medici, Marie 36, 59
de Ros, Lord 117
Dettingen, Battle of 50, 121
Dinner, Roger Monk 67, 80–1
Dudley, Yeoman Thomas 51

Edward I, King 68
Edward III, King 24, 65–6
Edward IV, King 21, 44
Edward VI, King 26, 80, 88, 120
Edward VII, King 16, 37, 55, 61, 76, 121, **11**
Edward VIII, King 64, 77, 121
Elizabeth I, Queen 18, 27, 39, 42, 48, 68, 81, 88, 93, 94, 95, 120
Elizabeth II, Queen 54, 58, 69–70, 78–9, 83, 99, 105, 107, 109, 110, 113–5, 121, **1, 15, 17, 19, 20**
Ensign 49
Ensign of the Guard 63, 77, 79, 83, 94–6, 102
Epiphany Service 67–8, 113, 125
Esquires 20, 36, 41
Exon of the Guard 36, 61, 63, 74–6, 80–1, 94–9, 105, 120, 122, **22, 24**

Falmouth, Viscount 33, 97, 120
Fawkes, Guy 71–6, 120
Ferrers, Lord 33
Field of the Cloth of Gold 56, 120, **2**
Field of Stoke, Battle of 44, 120
France 44–5, 50, 56–7, 92, 94, 96, 120
Francis I, King 45, 56, 88
Frye, Yeoman John 15, 116
Funerals, Royal 52–6, 93, 125

Garden Parties, Royal 114, 125
Garter, King of Arms 101–4, **27**
Garter, Knights of the 40, 65–6, 93
Garter Service 65–6, 113, 125, **18**
Gates, Sir John 34, 118
Gentlemen
at Arms 40, 55, 61, 63, 80, 81, 92, 106
Pensioners 34, 35, 93
Privy Chamber, of the 52–3, 93
Spears 34, 45, 92, 120
Ushers 35–6, 41, 67–8
George I, King 121
George II, King 33, 36, 38, 50, 72, 121
George III, King 37, 40, 55, 67, 82, 90, 121
George IV, King 58, 80, 86, 91, 97–8, 121, **9**
George V, King 53, 55, 58, 66, 69, 121, **10, 12, 13**
George VI, King 17, 23, 77, 101–4, 121
Gilbert and Sullivan 9, 23
Gorges, Sir William 29
Grandison, Viscount 82
Grete, Bernard 19
Grey, Lady Jane 34
Griffiths, Yeoman 34
Guilford, Sir Henry 48, 117

Hanover, House of 50–1, 82, 101–2
Hatton, Sir Christopher 82, 92–3, 117
Hawkins, Yeoman Thomas 46
Hawkins, Yeoman William 41
Hennell, Colonel 83, 86, 101, 121
Henry IV, King 40
Henry VI, King 21
Henry VII, King 6, 10–15, 16–22, 23, 25, 33, 34, 41, 42, 44–5, 52, 59, 84, 94, 96, 101, 120
Henry VIII, King 14, 18, 19, 21, 22, 23, 26, 32, 34–5, 41, 45–8, 52, 55, 56–8, 68, 84, 87, 88, 92, 94, 109, 120, **2**
Hewlett, Flight Sergeant 51
Hornung, Lt Colonel 87

Ilchester, Earl of 15, 118
Inspections, Body Guard 67, 76–9, 82, 83, 84, 113, 121
Investitures 64–5, 112, 113–5, 121, 125, **14**
Ireland 49, 50, 56–7, 81, 91, 94, 112, 121

127

James I, King 49, 71, 90, 94, 95, 99, 100, 101, 120
James II, King 50, 82, 95, 120

Kerridge, Yeoman 37, 38
Knevet, Sir Thomas 72
Knighthoods, abolition of automatic 99

Lea, Yeoman Thomas 51
Leighton, Robert 29
Lieutenant of the Guard 63, 94–6, 99, 105–7, 122, **9**, **19**, **20**
Life Guards 35, 51, 96
Limerick, Earl of 118
Lincoln, Earl of 44
Lloyd-George, David 65
London, John de 24–5
Lords, House of 61, 63, 71–6, 106
Lying-in-State, Royal 53–6, **12**, **13**

Macclesfield, Earl of 97, 101, 118
Maddockes, Yeoman William 26, 116
Marines, Royal 48, 51, 76, 109, 121
Marney, Sir Henry 17, 19, 45, 117
Marsham, Ferdinand 35–6
Mary, Queen 34, 48, 68, 88, 120
Mary, Queen of Scots 81
Mary Rose, The 47, 120
Maundy Service 67, 68–71, 113, 125
Maximilian, Emperor 56
Meals, Royal 39, 40, 56–7
Messenger Sergeant-Major 96, 107–9, 111–4, 122, **7**
Milton, Thomas 11
Monk, Roger 67, 80–1, 114, **22**
Monson, Lord 83, 118
Monteagle, Lord 71–2
Montague, Sergeant-Major 8

Napoleon III 60
Nearest Guard 16, 55, 58, 63
Neerwinden, Battle of 50
Nicholson, Margaret 37, 38
Norfolk, Duke of 11–12
Northumberland, Duke of 12
Norwich, Earl of 49–50, 117

Onslow, Earl of 78, 119
Organisation of the Body Guard 16–22, 49–51, 82, 92–100, 105–115, 120–1
Oxford, Earl of 12–5, 16–7, 18, 117

Parker, Yeoman 88
Parliament, State Opening of 37, 38, 52, 53, 61–3, 72, 97, 98, 114, 125, **1**
Partisans 22, 55, 89, 111–2, 114, **12**, **13**, **23**
Pay 18–22, 24–5, 45–6, 48, 58, 95, 98–100, 115

Payne, Yeoman William 82
Person, Yeoman John 44–5
Philip, Prince **1**
Phillips, Messenger Sergeant-Major 108
Police 31, 33, 43
Prince Royal **3**
Progresses, Royal 42, 88
Purchase of Appointments 28, 95, 99–100, 121

Queen's Flight, the **26**

Raleigh, Sir Walter 34, 93–4, 117
Randall, Yeoman John 45
Receptions, Diplomatic 38, 114, 125
Regency 76, 97, 121
Phys-ap-Thomas 11
Richard III, King 10–14, 120
Roses, War of 10–15
Royal Air Forces 28, 51, 109, **26**
Royal Horse Guards 51

St George's Chapel 55, 65–6, **18**
St James's Palace 31, 37, 61, 67–8, 76–9, 98, 101, 102, 109, 114, 121
St Paul's Cathedral 14, 93, **8**, **10**, **15**
Salisbury, Lord 71–2
Scotland 41, 56, 58, 91, 120, 121
Sea, Yeomen Service at 47–8
Seal, Body Guard 15
Search, The 63, 67, 71–6, 97, 106, 108, 125
Sergeant-Major 61, 71, 74–6, 107–8, 123–4, 125
Sidney, Sir Henry 49, 81
Simnel, Lambert 44
Somerset, Duke of 26, 34
Somerset, Sir Charles 18, 117
Spain 18, 48, 61, 81, 94
Spurs, Battle of 45
Standard of the Body Guard 14, 18–9, 45, 61, 77, 83, 88, 101–4, 121, **27**, **28**
Standard-Bearer 18–19, 94–6
Stanley, Lord Thomas 11–14
Stanley, Sir William 11–14
State Banquet 38, 61, 125
State Visit 38, 56–61, 113–4, 125, **16**
Steward, Lord 56, 82
Stuart, House of 49–50, 82, 88, 99
Suffolk, Duke of 88
Surrey, Earl of 58, 118
Seymour Sadler, Sir Thomas **24**

Talbot 12
Title, Body Guard 16
Tournai, Body Guard at 19, 45, 120
Tower of London 17, 21, 23–33, 44, 72, 94, 120

Constable of 17, 28, 29, 31, 33
Tudor, House of 10–15, 16–22, 82, 84, 86, 87, 91, 109
Turner, Yeoman George 41
Turner, Colonel VB 78, 87

Uniform, Body Guard 9, 18, 20, 21–2, 36, 39, 45, 48, 49, 55, 56–8, 67, 71, 75, 80, 81–3, 84–91, 107, 111–2, 114, 120–1, **10**
Yeomen Warders 23–33

Vandun, Yeoman Cornelius 46
Victoria, Queen 15, 16, 24, 52, 55, 59–60, 62–3, 74, 79, 83, 97, 99, 101–2, 121
Visit, State 38, 56–61, 113–4, 125, **16**

Waldegrave, Earl of 85, 118
Wales 11, 64–5, 91, 115
Prince of 49, 64–5, 76, 121, 125
Walpole, Horace 97
Warbeck, Perkin 44
Warrant, Royal 13, 14–15, 17, 19, 41, 50, 90, 97
Weddings, Royal 39, 125
Wellington, Duke of 7, 29, 50–1, 56
Westminster 29, 33, 55, 64, 71–6, 106, 108
Westminster Abbey 14, 16, 32, 52–3, 66, 69–71, 81
Wheelmen 52, 53, 54, 62, 72, **15**
Whitehall Palace 55, 69, 72
Wilhelm, Kaiser 79
William and Mary 82, 90, 121
William III, King 37, 50
William IV, King 50–1, 55, 76, 84, 86, 99, 105, **24**
Williams, Yeoman John 26, 116
Windsor Castle 40, 43, 55, 59–61, 65–6, 93
Windsor, House of 101–4, **28**
Wingfield, Sir Anthony 34, 45, 117
World War One & World War Two 43, 51, 83, 105, 109, 111
Wood Yeoman 37

Yeoman Bed-Goer 41, 108, 123–4
Yeoman Bed-Hanger 41, 108, 123–4
Yeoman of the Chamber 20, 27, 41
Yeoman of the Crown 20, 26, 95
Yeoman Clerk 29
Yeoman Gaoler 29, 32, **4**
Yeoman Porter 24–5, 27, 29
Yeoman Raven Master 30, **5**
Yeoman Usher 20, 21, 36, 81, 96
Yeoman Warder 7, 9, 17, 23–33, 79, 111, 120
Chief 25, 27, 30, **6**